The Drip Effect

The Drip Effect

Breaking Free From Hustle Culture

Jimmy Casas

Jessica Cabeen

ConnectEDD Publishing

Hanover, Pennsylvania

This publication is available at discount pricing when purchased in quantity for educational purposes, promotions, or fundraisers. For inquiries and details, contact the publisher at: info@connecteddpublishing.com

Published by ConnectEDD Publishing LLC
Hanover, PA
www.connecteddpublishing.com

Cover Design: Kheila Casas

The Drip Effect —1st ed. Paperback
ISBN: 979-8-9933701-4-9

Praise for *The Drip Effect*

Jimmy Casas and Jessica Cabeen have written another leadership masterpiece! In *The Drip Effect*, Casas and Cabeen deliver powerful wisdom and practical insights that challenge leaders to think differently about the impact of their daily actions. This book reminds us that leadership isn't about one grand gesture—it's about the consistent "drips" that shape culture and influence others over time. A must-read for any leader looking to elevate their impact. An absolute home run!

—Jordan Montgomery | Montgomery Companies, Performance Coach, Author, Speaker

Jess and Jimmy have written the book I didn't know I needed, giving us the permission we've all been waiting for to finally trade the "hustle" for our true potential as leaders, and most importantly, as people. Their heart for educators shines through, offering research-backed, manageable steps needed to pull even the most exhausted among us out of the chaos. Reading this motivated me to reclaim my time and show up as my best, most authentic self for the community I love and serve.

—Carmen Maring | Middle School Principal, Educational Leadership Adjunct Professor, National Distinguished Principal

The Drip Effect, by Jimmy Casas and Jessica Cabeen, is a must-read for leaders who have felt the quiet weight of constant pressure. As a high school principal, this book spoke directly to my core. It made me feel seen, understood, and less alone in the challenges of leadership. With a powerful blend of authenticity and research, Jimmy and Jessica name what so many of us experience but rarely articulate. I found myself repeatedly saying "yes!" as I turned the pages, even highlighting quotable lines I know I'll revisit again and again. More importantly, this book gave me something every leader needs: hope. It reminded me that my best is enough and equipped me with practical tools to navigate the complexities of leading with clarity and purpose.

—Meg Simon | High School Principal, Ohio

Anyone can say leadership is complex and busy. (And we all do!) But very few in our profession have been able to provide a simple pathway to being present. That stops now. Jimmy Casas and Jessica Cabeen have crafted something special, and it's for *everyone* who's feeling the constant pull of *everything*. *The Drip Effect* is filled with raw and relatable stories, practical strategies, and a framework that actually works. So leaders can create a more sustainable rhythm and rebuild what the hustle has eroded. Because leadership isn't sustained by intensity. It takes intention. And that's what *Drip Effect* Leadership will help you get really good at bringing!

—Dr. Brad Gustafson | Principal, Author, and Lover of Life

If you remember nothing else, remember this: fast leaders don't always lead well; present leaders do. *The Drip Effect* is the antidote to hustle culture that education has been waiting for. Cabeen and Casas don't just challenge the pace of leadership; they redefine it. With clarity, heart, and practical moves you can use tomorrow, this book will help you trade urgency for intention and busyness for impact. More importantly, it gently reminds us that who we are becoming matters just as much as what we accomplish. This isn't just a book you read; it's one you feel, reflect on, and then live.

—Scott Borba | Superintendent/Principal, CA

The Drip Effect is a powerful reminder that leadership isn't about doing more, it's about being more intentional with what we already do. Casas and Cabeen give leaders language for the patterns that shape their work through clear, relatable archetypes, and more importantly, a path to move beyond them. The rhythm of Pause, Clarify, Act, and Refine offers a simple, sustainable way to lead without losing yourself in the process. This book brings leadership back to what matters most—presence, people, and purpose. It shows how small, intentional actions create the moments that build culture and lasting impact. Add this to your **To Do** list if you want **To Be** better for everyone in your world.

—Dr. Joe Sanfelippo | Retired Superintendent, Author, Speaker

This is a leadership book for people who feel the pace of the work and know something isn't right, but haven't found a clear way to change it. Leaders can tire of the tempo, even if we don't always say it out loud. What Jessica and Jimmy have created offers a different way—a simple, practical rhythm that helps leaders slow down, lead with design, and stay grounded in who they are while completing the work. It is a steady reminder that how we lead matters just as much as the outcomes we are driving, and that the best leadership can move beyond the individual into the habits, culture, and systems of an entire team.

—Dr. J. Anderson | Executive Director, Missouri Association of Elementary/PK-8 School Principals

In a profession where the pace never seems to slow, *The Drip Effect* gives leaders permission to pause and lead with intention. This book speaks to the heart of sustainable leadership, reminding us that the small, consistent moments are what truly shape culture and impact lives.

> —Dr. Courtney H. Dickey | Principal, Ella Banks Junior High

As someone who is often "busy" at the detriment of myself, I was ready for a new perspective on productivity. What I wasn't ready for was just how much this book would impact me. I was blown away by how deeply it shifted my thinking, my drive, and even my sense of peace. In a world that constantly demands more, *The Drip Effect* gently slows you down just enough to remind you that there is strength and power in the quiet, in the small moments. I can't recommend this book enough.

> —Todd Nesloney | International Speaker, Author, and Director of Culture and Strategic Leadership, TEPSA

Most leadership books tell you to do more. This one tells you to stop. Not forever. Just long enough to remember who you are and why you started leading in the first place. Jimmy Casas and Jessica Cabeen have written something rare: a book that gets stronger the slower you read it. The coaching conversations are not hypothetical. They are the exact moments playing out in schools and organizations right now. The dialogue with Jasmine will stay with you because you will recognize every word of it. Every leader has been in that exact conversation and made that exact mistake. *The Drip Effect* framework is deceptively simple: Pause, Clarify, Act, Refine. Do not mistake that simplicity for easy. This book will challenge you in the best possible way. Every leader I know is tired. Every leader I know is carrying more than they were built to hold. This book does not ask you to carry more. It teaches you to set things down with intention so you can pick up what actually matters. I will be putting this in the hands of every leader I work with. Read it slowly. That is the whole point.

—Kelly Croy | Director of Innovation & Instruction, Port Clinton City Schools, Speaker, Author, & Host of the Wired Educator Podcast

As a principal, I know how easy it is to mistake constant motion for meaningful leadership. *The Drip Effect* reminds us that sustainable impact comes from leading with purpose and intention, not by simply doing more. This book challenges school leaders to slow down, reconnect with who they are becoming, and embrace the small, consistent actions that transform schools and the people within them!

—Dr. Rachel Edoho-Eket | Principal, Author, Speaker

This is the book leaders need right now. For anyone who feels like they are running as fast as they can, but it still is not enough, doing all they can but still feeling behind, or leading effectively on the outside while feeling depleted on the inside, *The Drip Effect* offers both clarity and hope. With a humane, practical alternative to hustle culture and a memorable rhythm of *Pause, Clarify, Act, and Refine*, this book helps leaders lead with more intention, steadiness, and presence.

—Jamie Downey | Vice President, Marketing, Cengage School

The Drip Effect is a timely and much-needed challenge to a culture that too often celebrates exhaustion while neglecting what matters most. In these pages, readers will find a powerful reminder that great leadership is not built through constant motion but on presence, purpose, and the small daily choices that shape lasting impact. Honest, practical, challenging, and deeply human, this book offers a refreshing path forward for anyone who feels trapped in the grind of doing more. If you want to lead with greater clarity, protect what matters most, and build a life of meaning rather than mere busyness, *read this book*. It has my highest recommendation!

—Thomas C. Murray | Director of Innovation, Future Ready Schools, Washington, D.C.

The Drip Effect, by Jimmy Casas and Jessica Cabeen, is a practical guide that emphasizes a powerful truth: experience alone isn't the best teacher; reflection on experience is. Drawing from their deep work coaching others, the authors present a simple, memorable framework: Pause, Clarify, Act, Refine, that is immediately actionable in real-world leadership settings. Since reading it, I've been using their reflection cycle myself and coaching educators with it, and it works. The book is highly adaptable for group study, individual reflection, or integrated into coaching conversations. It could even be leveraged as a foundation for a leadership retreat. Cheers to the authors for a useful resource for purposeful reflection!

—William D. Parker | *Principal Matters: The School Leader's Podcast*

I'm proud to call Dr. Jessica Cabeen a friend and have long admired her ability to put into words what so many leaders are feeling but struggle to express. In *The Drip Effect*, Jessica and co-author Jimmy Casas do what they do best: help leaders feel seen, understood, and supported while inviting meaningful reflection and growth. They thoughtfully challenge the pull of hustle culture and encourage leaders to be intentional about who they want to be, both at work and at home. This book is a powerful reminder that leadership is not about doing more, but about becoming more of who we are meant to be.

—Allyson Apsey | Educator, Speaker, and Bestselling
    Author

Jimmy Casas and Jessica Cabeen once again demonstrate their unwavering commitment to the education community in their newest book, *The Drip Effect*. Known for their relentless care and support for educators—and especially principals—Casas and Cabeen deliver a timely and practical resource that helps to address the multitude of challenges facing campus leaders across our country. Through insightful strategies and proven methods, this book equips principals with the moves they need to survive and thrive in today's demanding climate. *The Drip Effect* is more than a guide; it's a catalyst for professional and personal growth. The author's wisdom and experience shine through, offering actionable advice and encouragement to those who have chosen to dedicate their lives to the success of students. This book is an essential read for anyone seeking to make meaningful impact as a campus leader. I highly recommend this book for all educators and school leaders committed to fostering excellence and resilience within their communities.

—Billy Pringle, Ed.D. | TASSP Executive Director

For most of my career, I thrived on complexity and prided myself on having the ability to look at a tangled problem and instantly see the path forward. That pattern worked until I hit a "capacity" brick wall. When I moved into central office administration, the volume of demands made it impossible to continue leading the way I always had. There weren't enough hours in the day, and no amount of hustle was ever going to change that. If I couldn't learn to build capacity in others, I was not going to succeed in this role. I had to change not only my habits, but my entire understanding of what leadership was for. *The Drip Effect* is the framework I wish I had found sooner. It gave language to the trap I had fallen into and, more importantly, a clear and sustainable path out of it. The four movements — Pause, Clarify, Act, Refine — are deceptively simple. In practice, they are transformational. I have watched my leaders take calculated risks they would never have taken before. I have seen confidence grow in places where dependence once lived. My leadership is not smaller because I have learned to layer it, because it is actually exponentially more effective. This book is not about doing less. It is about doing what matters, in a way that actually builds the system around you. Any leader who wants to stop being the ceiling of their organization and start becoming the foundation of it needs to read this book.

—Emily Graham | Assistant Superintendent, Taylor School District

Jimmy Casas and Jessica Cabeen have written a book that is truly transformational for leaders. The Drip Effect is more than a leadership read, it is a necessary mindset shift for every leader in today's schools. Like a "trim tab" on a ship, this book reminds us that it's the small, daily, intentional "micro-moves" that ultimately create significant change in how we lead our schools and districts. As I read, I found myself deeply reflecting on my own leadership. At times, I was uncomfortable, recognizing past patterns in how I've led others. Yet, that discomfort quickly turned into growth as each chapter offered a powerful reframe and a forward-thinking approach to leading with a greater passion, purpose and plan. In a world that often glorifies urgency and doing more, this book calls us to something deeper. It invites us to lead with relentless courage, not by doing more, but by looking within, reframing our mindset, and leading in a way that allows our leadership to create meaningful impact for ourselves and others. Jimmy and Jessica remind us that leadership is not just about what we do, but about who we are and that is where true impact begins. *The Drip Effect* is impactful, motivating, inspiring, timely and deeply insightful. It is an investment in yourself and your leadership!

> —Carrie M. Yantzer | Executive Leadership Development Strategist, Colorado Award Winning Principal, District and State Leader

As an educator for forty years and a school leader for more than twenty-five, I spent far too many years prioritizing speed over accuracy, reflection, and connection. Too often, that led to mistakes, burnout, and a constant cycle of hustling and grinding without meaningful impact. In *The Drip Effect*, Jimmy and Jessica offer me, and so many other school leaders, a powerful blueprint for showing up with intention and being truly present for our students and staff. This book reminds us to slow down, listen, lead with love, and act with intention. In many cases, simply being heard can be healing for members of our village. Read this book more than once. Its lessons can help you avoid many of the mistakes I made in my career and become the kind of leader our schools need most.

—Salome Thomas-EL, Ed.D | Award-winning Principal, Speaker, Author

The Drip Effect by Jimmy Casas and Jessica Cabeen is a powerful reminder that effective leadership is less about doing more and more about being intentional with your time, energy, and impact. This book helps leaders reflect, refocus, and redefine their role so they can lead with greater purpose, clarity, and sustainability. Perfect timing for our current intense world!

—Dr. Andy Jacks | Senior Fellow NAESP, National Distinguished Principal, Author of *Discipline Win*

Impactful, sustainable leadership requires a skill set that practices the tenets of *The Drip Effect* framework. This book is a permission slip for leaders who are committed to redefining their leadership and reclaiming their lives and purpose. I encourage leaders to take the pause and read this book–it will change not only how you lead, but how you live.

—Dr. Sanée Bell | Educational Leader, Author, Speaker

The work of leadership isn't speed; it's service. *The Drip Effect* reminds us that real impact happens when leaders slow down long enough to serve the unfolding teachers as self-directed content experts. If you want a school where presence replaces pressure, and people matter more than motion, Cabeen and Casas show the way forward.

—Ken Williams | Artist, Unfold The Soul

I would describe this book in two sentences: *The Drip Effect* is a masterclass in shifting from the exhaustion of the "hustle" to the enduring power of intentional practice. It provides the essential tools for any leader who wants to replace the burnout of the sprint with a sustainable, joyful rhythm of impact.

—Jennifer Womble | Chair, Future of Education
    Technology Conference (FETC)

Dedication

From Jimmy: This book is dedicated to the educators who show up every day and give so much of themselves in service to others, making countless sacrifices for the students, staff, and families you serve, not out of obligation, but because you genuinely care and want to make a difference.

May this book serve as a reminder that your impact does not have to come at the expense of your health, your loved ones, or your well-being. May it help you find healthier, more sustainable ways to lead and serve, so you can continue making the difference you were called to make for years to come.

From Jessica: This book is dedicated to the staff, students, and families of Austin Online Academy and Austin Area Learning Center—thank you for the trust, the patience, and the daily reminders that meaningful work is built in small moments, over time.

And to Lexy and Lucy—you are a steady reminder of the purpose, presence, and joy behind it all.

> *"Commit to the Lord whatever you do,*
> *and he will establish your plans."*
> —Proverbs 16:3

THE DRIP EFFECT
Table of Contents

Foreword

There is a moment most leaders recognize but rarely speak aloud. It does not arrive as a dramatic collapse. It arrives in a parking lot after a long day or lying awake at 2:00 a.m. cataloguing what didn't get done, or standing in a hallway between one urgent problem and the next. The realization is this: *I am doing everything, and I am present for none of it.*

I know that moment. And when I opened *The Drip Effect*, I found something rare: a book that not only names that feeling with precision and grace, but offers a practical, humane, and deeply sustainable path through it, one that reclaims the leader's health, relationships, purpose, and joy alongside their effectiveness.

The revelation that stopped me came early. The authors offer it plainly: leadership is not a title, a strategy, nor a performance we perfect. *Leadership is a practice,* and like all practices, it demands intention, repetition, and rhythm. That sentence quietly dismantles the most destructive myth of modern organizational life: that the best leaders are the fastest, the most urgently available, the most relentlessly responsive. That the calendar overflowing with back-to-back commitments is evidence of impact rather than evidence of a system that has slowly consumed the person inside it.

One of the most courageous things this book does is treat the leader's physical and mental health not as a wellness footnote, but as the foundation on which everything else depends. The book opens with Meg, a decorated leader, college athlete, and award-winner, who was spending her evenings curled up on the floor, battling anxiety, panic attacks, and insomnia. "Hustle Culture" had not just diminished her leadership. It had quietly dismantled her health. Her story is the story of the "Hustle Trap", the belief that your value is tied to how much you achieve, not who you are.

We live in an era defined by speed. Decisions are expected quickly, responses immediately, and productivity constantly. Leaders are celebrated for their ability to move fast, to manage complexity, and to remain perpetually available. Yet beneath this culture of urgency lies a quieter cost—one that is often unspoken but deeply felt. The absence of pause erodes not only clarity, but also health, presence, and sustainability. Leaders become reactive rather than intentional, efficient rather than effective, and, over time, depleted rather than fulfilled.

The Drip Effect offers an alternative, not through grand reinvention, but through disciplined simplicity. Its four-movement framework, *Pause, Clarify, Act, Refine*, presents a rhythm of leadership that is both accessible and transformative. These are not steps to be completed, but small habits to be cultivated. Together, they form a cadence that slows the mind just enough to think clearly, ground decisions in purpose, and create a flow that feels not forced, but aligned.

If I were to describe this book to another leader, I would do so simply: *This is not just a book about leadership; it is an executive coaching practice for the modern world.* It does not add to the already overwhelming list of things leaders must do. Instead, it reshapes how they do what already exists. It meets leaders where they are—busy, stretched, and often reactive— and offers a way to lead with greater intention, clarity, and calm. More importantly, it restores something often lost in leadership conversations: joy. Not the fleeting satisfaction of accomplishment, but the deeper sense of alignment that comes from acting with purpose. When leaders adopt this rhythm, they do not merely become more effective; they become more present, more grounded, and more connected to the work they do and the people they serve.

In an over-indulgent world of instant gratification, we need leaders who are stable, healthy, and present. We need leaders who understand that their health is not a luxury to be attended to after the work is done, but the very engine that makes the work possible.

Leadership books tend to arrive in one of two modes: they inspire you for seventy-two hours, or they hand you a system that collapses under the weight of a normal Tuesday. *The Drip Effect* does neither. The leader who pauses before reacting, clarifies before acting, moves with purpose, and refines through honest reflection is not a slower leader. They are a stronger one: physically steadier, emotionally healthier, relationally richer, and a leader whose impact outlasts them because it was never dependent on their constant presence to survive.

Begin here. One drop. One pause. One intentional choice at a time.

—Jennifer Eakin Womble | Chair, Future of Education
  Technology Conference

PART I

Introduction

You Don't Have to Lead Fast to Lead Well

Is busyness making you a better leader?

On paper, Meg had it all together. She was a high-achieving school leader, a former record-holding college athlete, recognized as a Top 20 Leader Under 40, and once named Assistant Principal of the Year. She was a proud wife of a loving husband and mom to two kind, energetic little boys. To an outsider, she appeared to have it all—a positive, driven woman at the top of her game. But what people did not see was that, for much of the past year, she spent her evenings curled up on the floor, battling anxiety, depression, panic attacks, and insomnia.

By all standards, Meg was a hard worker, dependable, and had a reputation for being quick on her feet and getting things done. Despite her accomplishments, she could not escape the feeling that she was not enough. The truth is, like Meg, leaders everywhere are caught in the sprint. That is the sneaky trap of what we call the "Hustle Culture." It convinces you that your value is tied to how much you do or achieve, not who you are. In Meg's case, that feeling crippled her.

Who are you? Who do you want to be?

These questions sound simple, but they carry weight. Not because they're abstract, but because leadership rarely gives us the space to answer them honestly.

Who are YOU? Who do you want to BE? And what IMPACT do you want to make?

If you're reading this, chances are you're searching for something more. Something beyond how you're currently showing up at work and in life.

Your phone rings. Emails ping. Someone's waiting at your door with a "quick question." You've been on the go since 7:00 a.m., and your to-do list looks like a game of whack-a-mole.

You're leading—or are you? Are you really present?

If you consider yourself a leader, regardless of your role, we tip our hats to you. You are a gift to your profession, and more importantly, to the people you serve. Over time, these individuals won't remember every task you completed, every meeting you led, or every policy you developed. However, they will remember how you made them feel. Whether they felt seen. Heard. Valued.

Sometimes, we look back at old photos or posts, and we see ourselves smiling in some of the pictures with friends and family, but then we wonder, were there more photos we never got a chance to take, because we were somewhere else - mentally or physically? So now we are asking ourselves, what would these pictures look like if they reflected all of us?

Did we look tired from too many late nights? Was that smile masking a mental list of unfinished tasks? Were we really present or just physically there? Were we listening and leading with intention or just surviving the pace? Effective, sustainable leadership doesn't start with doing more. It starts with being. Before you move, respond, or decide, there's a quieter question worth asking: Who am I becoming in the speed of my days?

Those memories reveal a truth that often gets lost, not only in the constant rush of leadership but in the constant rush of life. How we show up matters just as much as what we get done. It's easy to get caught in *doing,* moving quickly, because you feel the rush to do, do, do! As you hustle through another day, reacting and making decisions on the fly as you strive to lead, what if you were to slow down, pause, and ask yourself, "Who am I and, more importantly, how do I want to be remembered?" What do you want others to say about you someday?

> *You were someone who knew their name, how to spell it, and even pronounce it.*
> *You were someone who showed up at their functions or events.*
> *You were someone they could count on.*

You were someone who took time to sit and listen.
You were someone they looked up to and considered a mentor.
You were someone who was fully there—present and invested in
them as a person.

Or, were you THAT person? Always busy, but rarely available.

Who are you? Who do you want to be?

The Drip Effect is about a simple but profound truth: just as steady drops of water can carve stone and fill a reservoir, effective leaders create lasting impact through small actions, at a steady pace. When we slow down, we think more clearly, lead more purposefully, and build cultures that thrive long after we're gone, developing people, deepening culture, and leaving a lasting impact through *who we are*, not just *what we do*. This means your next moves need not be dramatic or perfect. Just showing up as your authentic self is a drop. Over time, those drops matter.

When we lose sight of *who* we are, it's easy to get swept up in the *doing*: checking boxes, answering emails, chasing outcomes. Over time, that pace starts to feel normal, even noble. But hiding and lurking beneath the constant rush of doing to excel is the antithesis of the Drip Effect: Hustle Culture. We define "Hustle Culture" as the pressure to excel that causes us to drift from presence to performance. That's when the cracks begin to show, not because we aren't capable, but because we are in constant motion and carrying more than we were ever meant to hold.

The Cost of Constant Motion

What if the pace you are proud of is the very thing undermining your leadership?

For many leaders today, Hustle Culture feels like it sits at the intersection of acceleration and expectation. Every request feels urgent. Every meeting feels essential. Every task feels like it needs to be done yesterday. And the faster we move, the less time we have to think.

Before we know it, that sense of "now" urgency causes us to lose our way in a string of decisions. If we don't pause long enough to ask ourselves *who we are* and *who we want to become*, the hustle will decide for us. That sense of urgency feels like a trap, and it doesn't just exhaust you; it can also alienate others. When every hour becomes triage, we sacrifice connections for completing tasks. And although we know what you do makes small differences each day, we want there to be more of them for you. Having to constantly tend to those urgent emails can leave you feeling like you finished the day with boxes checked, but no sense of meaning. We know that feeling all too well. There were days when we believed we led the work, but didn't feel like we led the people. Some days, we failed to invest time in building trust. And other days, we found ourselves, like you, juggling a crisis or dealing with employee issues, staffing shortages, and project deadlines. Each moment deserves presence, but the pace demands efficiency. But ask yourself this question: "Are there days when you feel like you make dozens of decisions and complete numerous tasks, but still can't recall a single moment of genuine connection?"

That's Hustle Culture in real time: movement without meaning because we get caught up in the *doing*. And when motion becomes the measure of leadership, even your best efforts start to feel hollow. Hustle Culture comes with a price tag—emotional, financial, and relational. In education, business, hospitality, the food service industry, and beyond, we see the fallout everywhere: burnout, turnover, disengagement, and employees who lose themselves while trying to outperform everyone and be everything to everyone.

For many in leadership positions, the days can feel like an episode of the Oprah Winfrey Show, but instead of: "You get a car, and you get a car, and you get a car," you get: "Do you have a minute, do you have a minute, do you have a minute?" And the truth is, we often know it's not going to be a minute, but rather thirty minutes of our life we are never going to get back. When do we ever slow down? That constant reaction to others' needs is exhausting, and we are all paying a heavy price.

When we replace rest with constant reaction, the costs add up fast, both for organizations and for the people inside them. Hustle Culture tells us that busyness is a badge of honor. It whispers that our worth is tied to how much we do, how fast we move, and how many boxes we can check off the list. But here's the real truth: Hustle carries a hidden cost. It drains our emotional reserves, strains our relationships, and leaves us feeling like we're never enough.

In the book *Lead From Who You Are* (2026) Joe Sanfelippo shares how his morning to-do list would follow the same pattern: show up to school, turn on his computer, get a seltzer water, open email, respond to email, sign forms, walk the hallways, connect with people, and get into classrooms. Then it hit him. By the time he reached the things he loved most, walking hallways, connecting with people, and getting into classrooms, he was already in a poor mindset. Emails led to more emails. A late form led to frustration. A budget question led to worry. And then he'd walk into the hallway carrying that stress with him. What does your list look like in the morning? Does it follow a similar pattern? Do you find yourself reacting to a list of things that never seems to get shorter, no matter how fast you work to get them checked off? Examine your current list closely, and you will see what we have come to learn. Most of the items on that list (if any) are not moving the system. For many to-do listers, it is a way to justify our hard work, so we have something that shows us, "Well, at least I got a lot of crap done today." The problem is, there is always more "crap" waiting for us tomorrow. And to add one more dosage of reality, what does your to-do list look like when you get home, and does it keep you from what you love most—your friends, your children, your spouse?

So re-assess your **To-Do** list and instead ask yourself, "What is on your **To-Be** list?" Who do you want to be? We can't imagine "Hustler" landing on that list. Besides, hustle doesn't discriminate. It comes with no boundaries, and it will eventually cost you. Frankly, like many of our colleagues, we are speaking from personal experience. The hidden cost? Your health or your loved ones. Both are loser deals.

But Hustle Culture didn't emerge out of nowhere. It grew from a system once designed to protect workers. The eight-hour workday, introduced during the Industrial Revolution, promised balance: eight hours for work, eight for life, eight for rest. But somewhere along the way, that balance was lost, and the workday morphed into a nine, ten, and twelve-hour work shift. Productivity became the measure of worth, and the pace kept accelerating, and the lines between work and life for many blurred completely. The eight-hour workday became less about protecting workers and more about maximizing output. Fast forward to today, and Hustle Culture has taken this to an extreme. It's no longer about working smarter. It's about working longer, faster, and harder. The game has changed, and the promise of balance has been replaced with the pressure to find ways to do more. Many school and business leaders today continue to feel these same pressure points, and eventually they manifest in different ways, from emails linked to cell phones to the unwritten rule or feeling to always be "on call" and responsive. These small actions that leaders often view as being responsive, visible, and communicative can cause the lines between work and still working (from home) to blur.

American Institute of Stress (2025) points out that the problem isn't just the pace. It's the mindset. When we equate success with constant productivity, we lose sight of what really matters: our health, our relationships, and our sense of purpose. The article challenges us to redefine success, not as doing more, but as doing what matters most.

However, the fallout is becoming harder to ignore. The World Health Organization (2021) reports that long working hours are linked to a 35% higher risk of stroke and a 17% higher risk of heart disease. What was once framed as commitment now carries measurable consequences. The cost isn't just physical. It's financial. Burnout is estimated to cost the global economy hundreds of billions annually in lost productivity. But even that doesn't capture the full weight. The cost is emotional.

The cost is relational. Leaders are losing themselves in the grind, and their teams are paying the price.

Here is what we have learned: You don't have to move fast to lead well.

If the Hustle Culture is the trap, slowing down is the way out. Escaping the trap requires reclaiming time to think. Without reflection, we react. With it, we can lead again.

Reflection has become a scarce resource. In accelerated systems, a leader's calendar mirrors the culture's tempo: back-to-back meetings, endless notifications, no margin for thought, and relational inquiries that cannot be answered in an email or solved with a spreadsheet.

Eventually, efficiency eclipses meaningful connections. At work, we catch ourselves rushing conversations or completing tasks simply to get them done, not to get them done well. Busyness becomes the disguise we wear to look competent. But underneath, something more costly is happening: we are losing ourselves in the Hustle Culture. This is the downward spiral to MORE. More hustle, more of your time. And more items to do. But the problem with the hustle to do more is that it leaves less of you for the people at work you serve, less for yourself, and less for those who need you the most—your loved ones.

Why Slowing Down Creates Stronger Leaders

At first, the sprint feels manageable, even motivating. You tell yourself it's temporary: *Just get through this week. Just make it to the break. Just finish this project.* But somehow, the sprint never ends. The finish line keeps moving.

And then it happens. You stop feeling inspired by the work that once lit you up. You start counting hours instead of making the hours count. The smallest problems feel heavier than they should. You find yourself staring at the screen, not because you don't care, but because you've run out of capacity to keep caring at the speed of DOING versus caring at the speed of BEING. One is sustainable, one is not.

For many leaders, entering into that quiet and slowing down feels foreign. After years of running on adrenaline, calm can feel uncomfortable. The moment the urgency fades, uncertainty creeps in. *Who am I if I'm not fixing something?* Here comes that To-Do list again, rearing its ugly head. How many times have you completed a task only to notice it wasn't on your list, so you added it and then proceeded to immediately cross it off your list because you wanted credit for it? That "fix-it urge" to get more done is real, friends. Slowing down isn't about doing less. It's about doing what matters most, long enough for it to take root. The workday that was once designed to protect time for rest and renewal has been stolen from us, and that space has been replaced by Hustle Culture. When leaders reclaim their time, they rediscover their capacity to think clearly, connect deeply, and lead sustainably. To understand why slowing down matters, it helps to know what happens when we don't.

When the Sprint Becomes the Strategy

When you stop choosing on purpose.

We tell ourselves the pace is temporary. Just a busy week. A moment we'll catch up from. But it doesn't stay temporary. The sprint stretches us. That feeling of urgency lingers. And before we name it, it becomes how we lead. Not intentional. Not strategic. Just constant. Urgency isn't optional anymore. It's the expectation. Dr. Christina Maslach (2016) identified three signs of burnout that emerge after prolonged stress:

- Emotional exhaustion: Feeling drained, as though there's nothing left to give.
- Depersonalization: Growing cynical or detached from your work or the people you serve.
- Reduced accomplishment: Wondering whether what you do even matters.

If any of those sound familiar, you're not alone. Many leaders we support and coach shared that when we first began working with them, they had reached a point where their energy outpaced their ability to restore. The work didn't stop, but their spark began to dim. The discrepancy between your energy output and your ability to restore is what Hustle Culture feeds on...it's a cycle of depletion that has leaders DOING a lot, with no sustainable strategies to stop the sprint and restore the DRIP.

Organizational psychologist Adam Grant (2021) describes a related state: *languishing*. It's not burnout. You still have energy. It's not depression; you're not hopeless. It's the space in between, when life feels blah—empty, flat, joyless, and aimless. For many educators and leaders, the past few years have been a master class in languishing. The effort is there, but the joy is gone. You're showing up, but not fully alive in the work. In some cases, it looks like *quiet quitting*—mentally disengaged from the work, completing only the bare minimum requirements, rather than going above and beyond. When prolonged stress goes unexamined, it often shows up as emotional exhaustion, detachment, or a quiet questioning of whether the work even matters. Some doubt their impact. Others linger in the grind. And for many, disengagement eventually follows, not because they stopped caring, but because the pace made caring unsustainable.

That's the quiet danger of the sprint: it doesn't always end in collapse. It did for Meg, but for every Meg, there is someone else who is languishing and struggling to get through the busyness of the day. Sometimes, the energy leaks just empty you. To find the answer, you must stop sprinting long enough to refill what's been drained, to rebuild your reservoir of resilience.

We believe that if you embrace *The Drip Effect Framework*, described in this book, you can reclaim that reservoir, not just for yourself, but for the people you lead. It will reframe how you think, how you lead, how you live, and how you resist the constant pull of urgency. The framework gives you a rhythm strong enough to cut through the noise. Instead of chasing every fire, you follow a framework to slow you down. Instead of reacting to every demand, you *pause, clarify, act,* and *refine* every decision with intention. The payoff is significant. When you focus less on fires, you can shift your focus to lead with clarity, calm, and purpose. Remember, not every problem is yours to fix. Resist the urge.

When the Cracks Begin to Show

Remember, not every problem is yours to fix. Resist the urge.

Burnout, disengagement, and the warning signs we ignore.

One evening, a parent sat on the couch with their child, half-watching a movie and half-answering what felt like an "important email."

"Are you watching?" the child asked.

Ugh. It wasn't the first time the question had been asked, but it was the first time it really landed. Like so many professionals and leaders, this parent had fallen into a familiar pattern: pouring every ounce of energy into work, stressing over every decision, and coming home too depleted to make even the simplest one, like what to have for dinner. And the most painful part? Too often finding ourselves distracted just enough to forget to invest in our own loved ones. Sound familiar? The external load swelled, the internal power drained, and the cracks had begun to show. In that moment, the child wasn't really asking about the movie. They were asking for presence. The people who matter most don't need us to *do* more. They need us to *be* there.

And that's the heart of sustainable leadership: creating enough margin to build capacity— because capacity, not productivity, is the real leadership advantage. Think of The Drip Effect as a slow, steady, consistent flow, not clogged, rushed, or jammed. When the drops and the flow are even, you respond to life's demands with steadiness instead of shortness.

Imagine this: You're standing at the edge of a reservoir, the purpose of which is to store the water supply. The water level is calm and full, a quiet strength waiting to be released. But over time, small cracks begin to form in the dam. Slowly, water starts to leak out. The reservoir cannot fulfill its purpose when it's leaking. As the cracks increase, the water flows faster. Eventually, there's not enough water to meet downstream demand. That's what happens to our resilience when life's demands outweigh our capacity to handle them. We start strong, but if the cracks go unnoticed, our reservoir drains, and so does our ability to learn, lead, and live well. Yet, when those caring for the reservoir recognize the problem and set up scaffolding to address the cracks, a hope-filled future is created. That's what *The Drip Effect* Framework offers.

The Drip Effect Framework

A sustainable way to lead.

Hustle Culture promises impact through speed. But the faster many leaders move, the more disconnected they become—from their purpose, their people, and even themselves. The Drip Effect offers a different way forward.

It is the antidote to Hustle Culture: a rhythm of leadership designed to sustain both people and performance. When we began shaping this framework, our goal wasn't to create a new leadership theory. It was to build a rhythm leaders could sustain; a way of living and leading that strengthens performance without sacrificing people, purpose, or presence. Across schools, nonprofits, small businesses, and organizations, we've seen the same pattern: leaders care deeply, work tirelessly, and give endlessly, often without a rhythm that protects their energy or their impact. Without rhythm, we slowly begin to see cracks in leadership that become imbalanced.

> Lasting leadership impact is created through small, intentional actions, taken at a sustainable pace.

So here is a simple but powerful truth: just as steady drops of water can carve stone and fill a reservoir, lasting leadership impact is created through small, intentional actions, taken at a sustainable pace.

+ When we slow down, we think more clearly.
+ When we lead with intention, cultures deepen.
+ When we choose rhythm over reaction, impact lasts.

It isn't about doing less. It's about leading with rhythm and doing what matters, with more meaning. The Drip Effect is built on four intentional movements: **Pause → Clarify → Act → Refine.**

PAUSE
...with stillness

CLARIFY
...with focus

ACT
...with Purpose

REFINE
...with Growth

Most of us already know these concepts in theory. The challenge is living them in order. We skip the pause. We react, fix, decide, delegate, and move on, because movement feels productive. But speed without alignment leads to rework, and when this becomes the norm, it eventually leads to burnout. Remember, as we shared before, the eight-hour workday was originally designed to protect our time for rest, reflection, and renewal. Hustle Culture broke that promise. The Drip Effect offers a different cadence, slow enough to notice, steady enough to last, one intentional action at a time.

One word of caution. Each movement of *The Drip Effect* also has an enemy, known as the Archetypes. Think of these like check engine lights in your car. They can quietly begin to erode your vehicle, or in this case, an entire organization, when left unchecked.

These archetypes—*The Reactor, The Striver, The Controller, and The Dreamer*—give language to the patterns of behaviors we see in leaders. But they become dangerous when people begin to *live inside them* rather than *learn from them*. When a leader over-identifies with an archetype, it can limit them and bring unintended harm to both individuals and—when left unchecked—the broader culture.

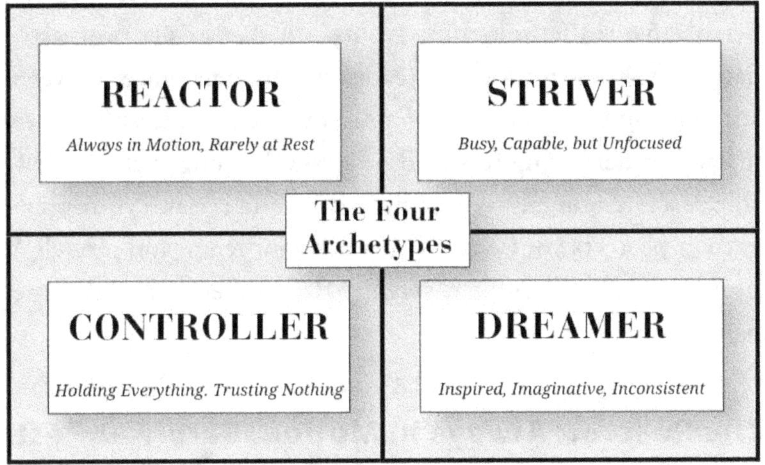

The goal isn't to eliminate these archetypes. Each one carries strengths:

- Reactors bring responsiveness
- Strivers bring a work ethic
- Controllers bring structure
- Dreamers bring vision

Archetypes aren't the problem. Unchecked patterns are. The moment a leader becomes aware of their default tendencies is the moment they regain the ability to lead with intention rather than instinct.

Let's break down The Drip Effect movements and the Archetypes you will find in the chapters ahead in greater detail:

PAUSE... with Stillness

Create space before you react. When everything feels urgent, perspective is the first thing we lose. A pause isn't procrastination. It's preservation. It creates just enough space between stimulus and response to choose your next leadership move instead of defaulting to speed or stress. Pausing is the leadership reset: a moment to breathe, notice, and reclaim your presence. It protects your energy, steadies your team, and models a healthier pace of problem-solving. Remember to practice the pause.

The Reactor: Always in Motion, Rarely at Rest

Reactors are driven by urgency. Defined by reaction. At first glance, they look like high performers. They're responsive, active, and always doing something. The problem is that constant motion becomes a substitute for meaningful progress. The organization becomes fast, but not effective.

CLARIFY...with Focus

Once you pause, clarifying has room to surface. Clarifying quiets the noise. It separates what is urgent from what is important, and reminds you what actually matters right now. It aligns your vision, priorities, and people. Clarifying comes from simple grounding questions: *What is this really about? What matters most? What's mine to do? Who belongs in this conversation?* Clarifying is not a one-time insight. It's ongoing alignment that guides every next step.

The Striver: Busy, Capable, but Unfocused

Strivers do more, but less that matters. They are often admired. They work hard, say yes often, and appear highly productive. But their effort is scattered, and their impact is diluted. In this environment, people may feel accomplished day-to-day, but disconnected from meaningful progress. The organization becomes full of effort, but short on results.

ACT...with Purpose

When you act from clarity, even the smallest drips create momentum, and others can join. You want action, but not a frantic, knee-jerk reaction. Move with intention. Movement without reflection becomes chaos, and reflection without movement becomes stagnation. Acting with intention means choosing progress over perfection and directing your energy toward what will truly move the work.

The Controller: Holding Everything. Trusting Nothing.

Controllers are in charge, involved, and overextended. They often believe they are ensuring quality and consistency. In reality, their need for control limits the very capacity they're trying to protect. Eventually, people disengage or become passive. The culture shifts from ownership to compliance, where people do what they're asked or told to do, but little more.

REFINE...with Growth

Refinement turns action into growth. It transforms mistakes into data-learning, frustration into feedback, and experience into wisdom. Instead of pushing harder, we pause to learn, adjust, and repeat. To refine is to ask: *What worked? What didn't? What needs to shift? And why? to all three.* The goal isn't perfection; it's presence. Every small adjustment strengthens your rhythm, your resilience, and your impact over time. It is the rhythm that keeps leaders agile, humble, and grounded. You don't need a new personality to lead well. You need a new rhythm.

The Dreamer: Inspired, Imaginative, Inconsistent.

Dreamers are full of vision, but short on follow-through. They bring energy, creativity, and possibility. They can rally people around ideas that feel meaningful and exciting. But without meaningful movement, vision becomes noise. Over time, inspiration turns into skepticism. People may nod along, but they stop believing.

When you lead through the **Pause, Clarify, Act,** and **Refine** framework, you create systems that run smoothly, and cultivate cultures grounded in trust, clarity, and purpose. It transforms urgency into alignment, busyness into balance, and pressure into purpose.

In the chapters to come, we will show you how each movement, when acted upon intentionally, builds on the previous, creating a rhythm that slows the chaos to a steady flow of droplets and strengthens your leadership over time. Each drop, each pause, each choice, each reflection, adds up. Over time, those small, steady rhythms don't just change what we accomplish. They change who we are and who we want to become.

Why Frameworks Matter

Frameworks don't restrict leaders. They release them. We've learned from our coaching work that frameworks help protect the reservoir. They are the scaffolding that ensures the cracks don't become gaping holes. Frameworks help treat the leaks, so every drip we pour into our purpose and people counts. When Hustle Culture tempts us to act urgently, a shared rhythm slows the pace just enough to prevent costly mistakes. Frameworks:

- slow us down long enough to think
- remind us to be more intentional
- clarify expectations
- make our leadership more predictable
- reduce emotional reactivity
- allow us to influence others in positive ways

Over time, this consistency reduces stress, instills confidence, and builds trust: people know what to expect and how we will respond. Predictability may not sound glamorous, but in leadership it's magnetic. When others know your rhythm, it sticks and they mirror it. That's how influence begins, not through control, but through replication and consistency. The Drip Effect Framework gives leaders and teams a shared process and language for leading with calm clarity in a world that rarely slows down.

How to Use This Book

Each section of this book will guide you deeper into one stage of the Drip Effect framework. Inside, you'll find:

- **Stories** from real leaders who first leaned into doing rather than being.
- **Research** that connects reflection to performance.
- **Prompts** that help you apply the ideas to your own leadership.
- **Practical tools** to build your rhythm right away.

Each chapter also offers practical ways to incorporate **micro-moves** into your day to help build meaningful momentum. Micro-moves are small, intentional actions that protect your rhythm in real life, especially when time, energy, and attention feel scarce. They are the steady drops that keep the reservoir full. Not dramatic overhauls. Not grand gestures. Just consistent, purposeful choices that compound over time. You'll learn techniques that restore clarity under pressure, from ten-second resets before tough conversations to daily reflection rituals that anchor your thinking. Two words that will help you be better for others today–slow down–will transform not just your own calm, but the emotional climate of your team.

You don't have to overhaul your life or leadership in a day. You just have to start. One drop, one intentional act that helps you pause, clarify, act, and refine. Over time, those single drops add up. That's the Drip Effect.

This is more than a book about leadership. It's a book about developing new patterns in your life before the hustle catches up to you. We hope that it inspires you to examine your thoughts, change your language, and impact your behavior so you can keep being who you're called to be, doing what you feel led to do, and remaining fully present wherever it is you're doing it.

Let's begin.

PART II

PAUSE...with Stillness

Replacing Motion with Intention

Who are you becoming in the speed of your days?

By now, you've seen the hidden cost of constant motion and the exhaustion that comes when you prioritize "do" before "who." But self-awareness alone doesn't change behavior. This section bridges the gap between insight and action. It explores the psychology of pace, the science of habits, and the simple shifts that turn exhaustion into endurance.

We don't lose ourselves all at once. We lose ourselves in the speed of our days. One quick response, one rushed decision, one more movement of choosing urgency over intention. Every time we say yes to the "gotta minute?" conversations, we start to see that what once felt like leadership starts to feel like survival. And the more we move like this, the harder it becomes to recognize who we're becoming. But speed without intentional pause isn't sustainable. And it's sloppy, reactionary at best. Sometimes, even a knee-jerk reaction. And it's a recipe for Hustle Culture, where those reactions can catch us, creating an undercurrent that can negatively impact team morale. The faster we move, the more likely we are to get sloppy and damage relationships, hurting the overall culture of our organizations. If the Introduction helped you understand *why* slowing down matters, this section shows you *how*.

Why Pause Matters

The leadership skill no one schedules, but everyone needs.

It's not about doing nothing; it's about becoming who you want to be while doing the *right* thing next.

> **Pause is the practice of stillness before strategy, creating just enough space between what happens and how you choose to respond.**

And for leaders who feel like they are expected to always be "on," always decisive, always moving, this can feel like the opposite of leadership. Pausing may look like hesitation. It may even feel like weakness. But if we're being honest, how has the constant speed of leadership been working for you?

Think of pause as the ability to interrupt autopilot so your actions align with your values, not your adrenaline. Because without pause, we don't choose, we react, and sometimes, over-react. And that reaction, no matter how well-intentioned, not only hurts us but also slowly shapes us into someone we never meant to become.

Pausing in Action

How one moment of stillness can change everything.

Pause isn't passive, it's perspective. It had been one of those days for Makayla, an assistant principal known for her calmness under pressure. But today, even she felt the weight: a parent complaint, a staffing shortage, a student crisis. By mid-afternoon, her in-box felt insurmountable, and her patience was thinning. When another tense email arrived, Makayla did what most of us would do. She started typing. The words were professional, but the tone was sharp. Her cursor blinked at the end of a sentence that felt more like a statement to be "right" than learning from another perspective. She hovered over *Send*, and then stopped.

Instead of hitting send, she stood up. She walked out of her office and down the hallway, peeked into a few classrooms, and let the rhythm of student life soften the edge of her frustration. Fifteen minutes later, she returned and reread the email. As she sat and stared at her words on the computer screen, she realized this is not who she wanted to be, but the words showed her who she was becoming, and it scared her. What she valued most, kindness and compassion, were missing in her message.

After a short pause, she rewrote the message with a softer approach and a tone of empathy instead of exhaustion and frustration. Immediately, she felt better. The next morning, she received an email from the parent thanking her for her thoughtfulness. That small pause shifted everything. What could have become a conflict became a connection.

In a world that often rewards urgency, stillness can feel almost rebellious. Yet, almost every meaningful shift in leadership begins there. Pause is the deliberate act of creating space before responding, of letting the noise settle long enough to hear what truly matters. Pausing does not mean you care less. It means you want to care *longer*.

> Pausing does not mean you care less. It means you want to care *longer*.

For Makayla, it was her values and her character that mattered most to her. By pausing, she responded in a way that reflected what mattered most to her.

What We Have Learned

What neuroscience tells us about clarity, regulation, and decision-making.

Daniel Kahneman's (2011) research on fast and slow thinking reveals a hard truth: most of our decisions are made before we've truly thought them through. System 1 is quick, automatic, and reactive—it helps us move, but not always wisely. System 2 is slower, more deliberate, and far less comfortable—it requires effort, attention, and intention. Most leaders don't lack knowledge. They lack the space to think. The pause is where System 2 gets a voice.

As leaders, we make thousands of decisions every day—far more than we can process with intention. With that volume, it's easy to see why we sometimes try to make *System 2* decisions using *System 1* speed. After all, a quick yes or no clears our desk faster than a thoughtful, "Let me check on that and get back to you."

The quickest answer isn't always the wisest one. And without pause, we don't just think faster, we think less. Imagine if, instead of getting caught up in the hustle, we slowed down long enough to say:

- *Let me reflect on whether this aligns with our mission, vision, and core values.*
- *Let's bring a few voices together to see how this might impact our students or staff.*
- Or even: *Is this sustainable, or just doable for today?*

Over time, leaders learn there is a rhythm to this work. Slowing down isn't hesitation, but it can feel that way for some leaders. For others, it can cause trepidation or even fear. And for others with whom we work, they shared that their issue wasn't being scared of slowing down, but rather how to pause when the needs and demands of others keep pouring in. How we bring our best selves and our values to the moments when we might be most vulnerable is what matters.

That rhythm becomes especially clear while looking at what happens when a pause is missing. In the following section, we will examine our first archetype, the *Reactor*, to show us what leadership looks like when motion replaces meaning, and how stillness can restore both.

The Reactor Archetype

Always in motion. Rarely at rest.

The day starts before sunrise, and before you've even settled in, the race has already begun. Emails, texts, unexpected visits, hallway questions, and the ever-present "Got a minute?" pull you in ten directions at once. You're moving fast, solving problems, answering calls, and filling gaps. By the end of the day, you feel like you accomplished a lot, but you can't quite name what moved the work forward or if it even moved at all.

This is the world of The Reactor, the leader whose value feels tied to motion. The Reactor thrives on momentum, often mistaking busyness for purpose and speed for effectiveness. The Reactor's attention is constantly divided, their energy scattered across competing demands. Urgency becomes the default setting, and presence—the ability to truly see, hear, and think—gets lost somewhere in the rush.

But beneath all that motion is often something deeper: anxiety masquerading as productivity. Reactors believe that if they just keep moving, nothing will fall apart. Yet the faster they go, the more fragmented their leadership becomes. Their team learns to bring every problem to them, reinforcing a cycle of dependence and exhaustion. The irony is that we then turn around and complain to others about how exhausted we are from having to take care of everyone else's problems. The work is demanding. That's true. But when everything routes through you, you're not just responding to urgency—you're multiplying it

Pause is the antidote to the Reactor's restlessness. Pausing isn't passive. It's how we reclaim focus. Every time we split our attention, we dilute our impact. The pause reminds us that presence is the real productivity.

During our first meeting with Jordan, he shared that he was the kind of leader others described as "always there." He arrived before sunrise, answered emails while checking his messages, and held impromptu problem-solving sessions in every hallway he walked. If something needed fixing, Jordan was already halfway to the solution before anyone finished explaining the problem. People admired his

> Pausing isn't passive. It's how we reclaim focus. Every time we split our attention, we dilute our impact. The pause reminds us that presence is the real productivity.

responsiveness. He privately feared what would happen if he ever stopped moving.

Most days, Jordan ricocheted from crisis to crisis to calendar invite, collecting a series of half-finished tasks and mental Post-its along the way. By the time dismissal rolled around, he often felt wrung out, yet his mind continued to race. Beneath all that motion, he described a quiet narrative that is all too familiar to many leaders with whom we work: *If I slow down, everything will unravel. If I take a minute, I'll fall behind. If I pause, people will think I'm not committed.*

Jordan shared an experience he had one day that captured it perfectly. Before he even reached his office:

- A counselor chased him down about a student issue
- Transportation called about a bus referral
- A teacher stopped him in the parking lot
- His superintendent texted him about a board presentation

By 9:30 a.m., Jordan felt like he had already worked a full day. That's when the words floated back to him, something we'd discussed during a coaching session months before:

"When you act as though everything is urgent, Jordan, you send the message that nothing is actually important."

Jordan could feel the day getting away from him, so he paused. Just for a beat. He ducked into his office, closed the door, a radical act for a Reactor, and asked himself a question he rarely made space for: "What is the real work today?"

Not the loudest work.

Not the easiest work.

Not the work that made him feel useful.

The real work.

In that moment, he did something different. He listed every demand swirling in his mind and circled the only one that aligned with his long-term priorities. Everything else could wait, be delegated, or scheduled later. Jordan had found his quiet peace:

+ He asked the counselor to handle the student conflict.
+ He delegated the transportation issue.
+ He scheduled the teacher conversation for later.
+ And he blocked ninety uninterrupted minutes to work on the strategic plan he hadn't been working on, but needed to be worked out.

The surprising part? The world didn't fall apart. No one questioned his commitment. People thanked him for giving them ownership. For the first time in months, Jordan felt present instead of scattered.

He learned that pausing didn't slow the work down. It stabilized it. It didn't make him less available. It made him more effective. And it reminded him of a truth he

> When you create space to think, you create space to lead.

had forgotten in his season of relentless urgency: When you create space to think, you create space to lead.

That kind of pause isn't complicated, but it is intentional. And in moments when everything feels urgent, it requires us to interrupt that pattern. **The Reactor Reset:** When you find yourself slipping into the Reactor Archetype:

- Stop the motion. *Literally pause, no typing, no walking.*
- Name the moment. *I'm reacting, not leading.*
- Ask one question. *What is the real work right now?*
- Choose one move. *Delegate, delay, or do, with intention.*

Not perfectly. Just deliberately.

Pause Cues

Creating space before you react.

The term "Pura Vida" (1956) was first used in the 1950s in a Mexican film that was popular in Costa Rica. The country had just abolished its army, and the term soon became a symbol of the country's peaceful way of life. It was a time when Costa Ricans began to embrace a simpler lifestyle. Pura Vida, translated literally, means "pure life," but its meaning extends far beyond its literal definition. Costa Ricans embrace Pura Vida as a way of life. Instead of pursuing a fast-paced lifestyle, Costa Ricans prioritized happiness and fulfillment. This approach to life encourages individuals to slow down and appreciate the present moment, believing that work should be fulfilling and enjoyable. In a world that's constantly on the go, this approach can bring a sense of peace and contentment to daily life.

The ancient Chinese proverb states, "The best time to plant a tree was twenty years ago. The second- best time is now." It encourages us to take immediate action rather than dwelling on past inaction or missed opportunities. So, perhaps yesterday was the best time to slow down, but the second-best time is today. By slowing down and savoring every experience, we can cultivate gratitude and a deeper connection to the world around us. The "Pura Vida" mindset teaches us to let go of stress and worry and focus on what truly matters. It's about finding balance and making time for the things that bring us happiness and fulfillment.

Micro Moves That Matter

Leadership rarely shifts through grand gestures. It changes in the small, steady moments when we choose presence, focus, and progress, rather than perfection. *Micro moves* help us reframe not only the way we see our organization, but more importantly, help us maintain a steady perspective to ensure a better response. They remind us that no single raindrop is responsible for the flood. *Micro moves* are the everyday decisions that, repeated effectively over time, reshape culture and create meaningful change.

Having served in school leadership for more than a combined forty years, we know the work can feel overwhelming. In no way would we ever try to simplify or minimize those feelings that can cause even the most confident, positive leader to question themselves. We've internalized those same feelings many times over the years:

There's no way I'll get this done.
Does any of this even matter?
I don't think I'm the person for this.
I am not sure where or how to even begin.
I am just tired.

Working toward something meaningful often feels impossible in the middle of the process. That's why The Drip Effect is more than a leadership model; it's a mindset. It's how we break the impossible into the incremental, so we can move past that overwhelming feeling that can leave us feeling paralyzed. The framework serves as a tool to help us consistently stay focused on the *one thing*, rather than *everything*. Small, consistent, deliberate steps—**micro moves**—become the quiet engine of sustainable growth. This is what researchers and high-performing teams often describe as *marginal gains*—the idea that small, consistent improvements, compounded over time, lead to extraordinary results.

This isn't just theory. It's been proven in high-performance environments. The British Cycling Team in the early 2000s is a now-famous example. For nearly a century, they hadn't won a single Tour de France. Then came a simple philosophy. The aggregation of marginal gains; the belief that improving everything you do by just 1% can create extraordinary results over time (Clear, 2018).

Under Performance Director Sir Dave Brailsford, they examined every detail, from bike ergonomics and aerodynamics to sleep quality and hand-washing. Each singular change was tiny. Together, those changes transformed the team into a global powerhouse. That's the power of micro moves: small, sustained improvements that stack into significant transformation. One drop, one choice, one day at a time.

The same principle applies in leadership. When something feels overwhelming, the instinct is to look for a breakthrough. But sustainable change rarely comes from one big move. It comes from the next right one.

Pause and ask yourself: *What feels most overwhelming right now?* When the goal feels too big, whether it is improving culture, rebuilding trust, or restoring morale, don't search for a grand solution. Identify one small, intentional action that moves it forward.

Over time, these micro-moves become marginal gains. And those gains create what matters most in leadership: **mattering moments**—the moments when people feel seen, supported, and valued. Those are the moments that shape culture. Those are the moments people remember. Micro moves improve how we lead. Mattering moments define who we are as leaders.

Processes and strategies can build efficiency; only connection builds belonging. Mattering moments remind us that leadership isn't just about outcomes. It's about people. Every time we pause to listen, every word of encouragement, every intentional check-in and circle back to close the loop builds trust and fuels the connected culture we want to create. These small, human-centered

> Micro moves improve how we lead. Mattering moments define who we are as leaders.

choices are where impact begins. They don't slow the work down; they make the work matter.

Mercurio (2023) explains that anti-mattering is often at the root of what we label as motivation or behavior problems. It's not that people stop caring. It's that they stop feeling like they matter. He shares the story of a maintenance worker whose daily task was to wash first-floor windows. When she proposed a simple fix that would save hours of work, her supervisor replied, "That's not your problem. Just do your job." She didn't stop working. But she stopped caring.

The Drip Effect framework ensures that your actions and intentions reinforce how much you matter and help you show up in a manner that ensures others feel like they matter, too. Which is deeply important, because the risk of not doing so is "anti-mattering." That's what anti-mattering does. It drains energy, erodes trust, and silences contribution. The solution is remarkably simple: create consistent moments of mattering: small, intentional acts that remind people they're seen, valued, and essential to the mission. Mattering doesn't require more time, just more intentional pauses. Small, steady gestures of recognition can turn ordinary days into an extraordinary culture. Leadership expert Dan Heath, in his book *"Upstream,"* (2020) describes how we often spend our energy rescuing people from the river instead of walking upstream to prevent them from falling in. The same is true in leadership. When we live in constant reaction, answering every email, solving every crisis, we're managing *symptoms*, not *systems*. The Pause is what allows us to walk upstream. It gives us the vantage point to notice patterns, prevent fires instead of putting them out, and lead from foresight instead of fatigue.

So, now what? If you are like the two of us, chances are you've experienced being a *Reactor* at some point: running around, putting out fires instead of preventing them. Shifting how you respond to requests is one of the simplest ways to build *pause practices* into your day.

Micro Moves for Meaningful Momentum

Simple practices to slow the swirl and choose with intention.

PAUSE — Create Space Before You Respond

Guiding Question: *What truly matters right now?*

Purpose: Interrupt urgency long enough to choose with intention. Pause slows the swirl so you can respond from your core values instead of adrenaline. Learning to listen before leading.

Prompts: Choose one. Pause doesn't require all four:
- What is the real issue beneath the noise?
- What am I reacting to instead of reflecting on?
- What would success look and feel like for others, not just for me?
- What is the cost of acting now instead of acting wisely?

Outcome: A leader who leads their response—choosing clarity over reflex and intention over urgency.

What This Looks Like in Practice

Small shifts. Immediate relief. Long-term returns.

- A reflective moment at the end of a meeting. Each person names out loud what truly moved the work forward, and what simply filled time.
- A short walk outside before sending a difficult email, letting adrenaline settle so tone matches intention.
- A morning ritual to protect your peace, sitting in silence, deep breathing, journaling, meditation, prayer, or gratitude, that grounds you before the day's demands.
- A Friday "stop-doing" review: *What did I do out of habit instead of purpose?*
- A short journal entry at the end of each day that states your wins, where you fell short, and what you learned from it. But be sure to start with your wins because you have them every day even when it feels like you didn't.

When reframed, we can turn ASAP–*As Soon As Possible*–to *As Slow As Possible*. This is not negligence, but necessary. These small acts of stillness are taken intentionally to interrupt the reflex of hustle. They enable you to choose a response instead of reacting from exhaustion.

Your Next Move

What happens when leaders stop reacting and start leading.

By nature, leaders are wired for high capacity. Over the years, we have learned that every day brings a different rhythm, and we must pause to see when to lean into those rhythms and know when to retreat. The key is self-awareness. Where do you *need* to be right now versus where do you *want* to be right now?

> **Stop** *believing constant motion equals effectiveness.*
> **Start** *trusting that less speed creates a deeper impact.*

We see this often in our work as leadership coaches. It is not uncommon for us to see a building principal get sucked into the day's pace, which makes them feel like they are losing the day. Having both served in the role of principal for many years, we know from personal experience that it is easy to get caught in that swirl. One principal in particular shared how he hadn't been in any classrooms in three weeks because of a high number of student discipline issues in his building. It is important to note that he had identified this as an area he wanted to improve, given his past pattern of not consistently getting into classrooms. He shared privately that his priorities were impacting student achievement, aligning the curriculum, and ensuring his teachers felt supported, and he felt a sense of guilt for not following through.

During our conversation, he admitted that he felt more comfortable in his role dealing with student behaviors than he did in leading instruction. In this case, where he *wanted* to be took precedence over where he *needed* to be. Coaching him to slow down, pause, and reflect on aligning his practices with what he had shared he valued most, his staff, we were able to get him back on track before our next visit. He learned that pause doesn't take a special talent, it just takes practice. When leaders build pause practices into their rhythm, they strengthen their capacity to:

+ See people before problems.
+ Name what matters before moving forward.
+ Align decisions with core values instead of urgency.

One difference we consistently see between effective leaders and really effective leaders is the one who slows to pause before they respond is often the one who gets better results.

Pause is the foundation of every other rhythm in The Drip Effect. Without it, *Clarify* becomes cluttered, *Act* becomes chaotic, and *Refine* becomes rushed. Pausing doesn't slow progress. It sustains it, and more importantly, allows you to see that a leader in constant motion is simply a reactor in practice.

> One difference we consistently see between effective leaders and really effective leaders is the one who slows to pause before they respond is often the one who gets better results.

PART III

CLARIFY...with Focus

Separating Purpose from Pressure

PAUSE
...with stillness
CLARIFY
...with focus

What deserves your focus? And what is simply demanding your attention?

Most leaders don't lack effort; they lack focus. We care deeply, work tirelessly, and give endlessly, but without clarity, our energy scatters. We say yes to everything and move a thousand things an inch, instead of moving the right things forward in significant ways.

Clarifying is the bridge between pause and action. If *Pause* helps us step out of the swirl, *Clarify* is the discipline of narrowing focus so effort aligns with purpose—not pressure. It turns motion into momentum, activity into alignment, and effort into impact. But here's where this shows up in real leadership:

A principal walks into the day with a full calendar, but no defined priorities. By 10:00 a.m., they've responded to emails, handled a student issue, covered a class, and attended a meeting, but haven't touched instructional leadership, the very thing they said mattered most.

A teacher leaves a team meeting unclear on what was actually decided, so they spend the next week checking in, second-guessing, and reworking plans that were never fully aligned. A leadership team says "yes" to another task or initiative, not because it's the most important work, but because no one clarified what should come off the table first.

This is how decision fatigue compounds. Not through one major decision, but through hundreds of small, unexamined ones. And over time, leaders begin to feel it:

+ The constant mental switching
+ The pressure to respond quickly

- The quiet frustration of being busy without moving anything forward

This is where many leaders misdiagnose the problem. They assume:

"I need to be more efficient."
"I need better time management."
"I need to work harder to keep up."

But this isn't a time problem. It's a clarity problem. And when clarity is missing, something subtle, but significant, begins to happen. Leaders don't just lose focus; they lose trust in their own decisions:

You start second-guessing choices you already made.
You revisit conversations that should have been resolved.
You leave meetings wondering if everyone heard the same thing you did.

Not because you're incapable, but because nothing was ever fully clear to begin with. Over time, this creates a quiet erosion. Decisions take longer. Conversations feel heavier. And even small choices begin to feel disproportionately difficult.

This is where leaders often compensate in ways that feel productive, but actually make things worse. This shows up as over-explaining, over-attending, and inserting themselves into more conversations than necessary. This is not because they want control. It is because they are trying to create clarity after the fact—and how exhausting is that for leaders?

Gentle reminder here: clarifying doesn't come from revisiting everything. It comes from defining what matters before everything begins. When that doesn't happen, leaders find themselves stuck in a loop: Respond → Rework → Re-explain → Repeat

And each time through the loop, the work feels heavier. This is where many leaders begin to feel overwhelmed, not by volume, but by ambiguity. Because ambiguity demands constant interpretation. And interpretation drains energy faster than execution ever will. When leaders don't clarify what matters most, their teams feel it, too.

Here is how that can start showing up: The team starts to hesitate. They wait for direction. They check and recheck before moving forward. Not because they lack initiative, but because they don't want to get it wrong. And slowly, momentum stalls. And this doesn't come from resistance, but rather uncertainty. This is why clarity is not just a personal discipline; it's a leadership responsibility.

Because when leaders name what matters most, they don't just create direction, they create permission. Permission to move, to decide, and to lead.

Because when priorities are unclear, everything feels equally urgent. And when everything feels urgent, leaders try to hold everything. That's where the real drain begins. Because when clarity is missing, leaders don't just make more decisions. They make lower-quality decisions under pressure. They default to what's loudest, newest, and easiest to respond to, instead of what's most aligned, most impactful, and most necessary. And here's the tension most leaders don't say out loud: Being responsive feels like leadership. But responsiveness without clarifying is just a reaction with a title. Clarifying isn't a personality trait. It's a discipline. It requires leaders to:

- Decide what matters most *before* the day begins
- Revisit priorities when new demands appear
- Say no, delay, or delegate when something doesn't align

And this is where it gets uncomfortable. Because clarifying forces trade-offs. You can't prioritize everything. You can't respond to everything. You can't carry everything. So leaders either choose to move with intention or drift into reaction. When clarity is present, the entire system shifts.

Leaders:

- Spend less time deciding and more time leading
- Move from scattered attention to sustained focus
- Feel less urgency—even when the work is complex

Teams:

- Know what matters most
- Make decisions without constant approval
- Build momentum instead of waiting for direction

And perhaps most importantly: Leaders begin to feel a sense of control without needing to control everything. Clarifying is not about simplifying the work. It's about simplifying what you give your attention to within the work.

Because leadership will always be complex. There will always be competing demands. But clarity gives you a way to move through that complexity without losing your direction.

Why Clarify Matters

How misalignment fuels exhaustion.

> **Clarifying is the discipline of deciding what does and what does not deserve your effort.**

Without clarifying, even strong leaders drift. We stay busy, responsive, and well-intentioned, yet disconnected from the work that actually moves the mission forward. Calendars crowd. Energy scatters. Decisions multiply without direction. Focus is not neutral. What leaders choose to attend to and not attend to, especially under pressure, shapes outcomes more than intention ever could.

It was clear that Jasmine, a district leader, was frustrated, but the cause was unclear:

Coach: It's OK, Jasmine. I am grateful you feel comfortable sharing your frustration with me. If you had to pinpoint it, what do you think you are most frustrated about right now?

Jasmine: I stopped by the high school today to check on how the data walks were going. While I was there, I was stopped by the union representative, who was angry that administration did not notify teachers that they were going to be in their classrooms.

Coach: *How did you respond?*

Jasmine: *I told him we had discussed this at our principal's meeting and that they should have been notified ahead of time to avoid this very issue. I apologized and told him I would follow up with the principal to understand what had happened.*

Coach: *Did you and how did that conversation go?*

Jasmine: *Well, yes. Not well.*

Coach: *Tell me more.*

Jasmine: *She shared with me that she felt undermined and not supported because I had assumed that she had not communicated with her teachers when, in fact, she had. She was also frustrated because I hadn't redirected the union rep back to her.*

Coach: *Do you think she had a right to be frustrated with you?*

Jasmine: *I don't know. I am just tired and frustrated that I always seem to be dealing with issues at the high school. I don't have these issues at our other schools.*

Coach: *Are you saying you are frustrated with the high school principal?*

Jasmine: *I guess. I don't know. I was just trying to help because this is not the first time the union representative has come to me.*

Coach: It's OK. Do you want to talk about it more so we can clarify what is causing your frustration?

It is not uncommon for us to find ourselves in similar conversations when coaching leaders across the country, regardless of their role. We eventually were able to determine the root of the frustration. There were three things that Jasmine took away from our conversation:

1. She was upset at herself because she knew better than to put herself in the middle of this issue, but felt pressured to respond to the issue and try to address it in the moment.

2. She had created a pathway of complaints from the union representative to herself that now demanded her constant attention and time, which took her away from her own work.

3. We determined that there were underlying trust issues between her and her principal that had not been addressed. These issues had grown over time based on Jasmine's previous experiences when the principal had indeed failed to clearly communicate effectively.

When clarity is lacking, leaders can unintentionally default to urgency, assumptions, and over-functioning. The work loses direction, consumes time, and in this particular case, it eroded trust. When clarity is present, decisions feel lighter. Teams move with confidence. Effort compounds instead of competing with itself. Clarify protects leaders from becoming busy and over-striving and ensures effort serves purpose, not pressure.

And one final takeaway that day from our work with Jasmine, and a reminder to all leaders: Not every problem is yours to fix. Resist the urge. When we clarify the journey we are on together and learn from one another's collective experiences, we can turn those lessons into a slow drip of productivity.

> Not every problem
> is yours to fix.
> Resist the urge.

Clarifying in Action

How one clear priority reorders everything.

Clarity doesn't arrive all at once. It arrives in moments of honest decision.

It was scheduling season, and Miguel, a middle school principal in his fifth year, found himself swimming in spreadsheets, staffing lists, and competing priorities. Every conversation felt urgent: teachers wanted clarity on schedules, district leaders wanted updates on data, and families wanted communication about next year's changes.

By the end of the week, his to-do list had become a tangle of tasks and half-decisions. He was scattered, exhausted, but worse yet, he had talked himself into believing that this was the way it needed to be each spring. That afternoon, he reached out to his mentor for advice, who asked him a simple question: *"Of everything on your plate, what matters most right now?"*

Miguel hesitated. Then, slowly, he named it: building trust with staff during change. The moment he said it out loud, the fog began to lift. He postponed two meetings, rewrote the agenda, and met with a team of teacher leaders to clarify the "why" and seek out critical feedback on scheduling shifts. By Friday, instead of chasing a dozen fires, he reignited his focus, and the team followed

> Clarifying doesn't reduce the workload. It reorders it.

suit. Clarifying doesn't reduce the workload. It reorders it.

That's the quiet power of Clarify. When focus is named, actions start to drip, and those purpose-filled drips add up. When the purpose is clear, teams align. Leaders don't do less; they do what matters most.

What We Have Learned

Why distraction, not difficulty, drains leaders.

Leadership today demands constant decision-making, often in environments marked by interruptions, urgency, and noise. Over time, that fragmented attention erodes strategic thinking. Leaders respond faster, but see less.

Psychologists describe this as decision fatigue—the decline in decision quality after repeated choices. The more decisions we make, the harder it becomes to think clearly, weigh trade-offs, and act with intention. But here's what often gets missed: It's not just the volume of decisions that drains leaders. It's the number of unnecessary decisions created by a lack of clarity. Every unclear priority creates more decisions than it solves.

Research by Evan Polman and Kathleen Vohs (2016) adds an important layer to this understanding. Their work shows that decision fatigue is influenced not only by how many decisions we make, but also by whether those decisions align with how we see ourselves as decision-makers.

In their study, individuals who tend to view themselves as independent—those who naturally take ownership and make decisions confidently—reported feeling *less* depleted when making decisions for others. In contrast, individuals who are more interdependent—those who value collaboration and shared responsibility—experienced greater fatigue when required to make decisions alone.

In other words, fatigue is not just about effort. It's about alignment. This helps explain why some leadership moments feel energizing while others feel exhausting, even when the workload looks similar. When leaders are consistently asked to make decisions that don't match how they are wired to lead, the drain intensifies. And this is where clarity becomes critical.

Another way to understand this is through how leaders use their strengths. When leaders are consistently asked to make decisions that don't align with their natural leadership style, the drain intensifies. Some leaders feel energized by taking ownership and making decisive calls, while others are energized through collaboration and shared decision-making. When those patterns are disrupted, fatigue sets in, not because the work is too difficult, but because it is misaligned.

As Jessica shared in *Principal in Balance* (2023), the greatest risk of decision fatigue isn't making the wrong decision. It's losing the energy to decide at all. And most of that exhaustion doesn't come from complexity. It comes from deciding things that were never clearly defined in the first place. Seeking clarity doesn't increase effort. It reduces distraction.

When leaders define what matters most, fewer choices compete for mental energy. Focus sharpens. Insight improves. The work becomes intentional instead of reactive. In practice, clarity functions as a cognitive filter. It helps leaders determine what deserves sustained attention and what does not. Without that filter, responsiveness gets mistaken for effectiveness. Leaders answer everything, but advance very little.

As we've seen in our work with school leaders, clarifying doesn't eliminate complexity. It makes complexity manageable. It gives leaders a way to navigate competing demands without losing sight of what matters most.

The Striver Archetype

Busy. Capable. Unfocused.

Strivers don't lack commitment to do more. They lack containment. Driven leaders often confuse responsiveness with leadership. They support everyone, fix everything, and rarely slow down long enough to notice that motion has replaced meaning. The pace feels necessary, even virtuous. Fixing "it" is like consuming "it." When the Striver within us is presented with an issue to fix, we feel obligated to do so. It's our job, after all—or we convince ourselves that it's our job. But happens when we can't or we think we did, but we didn't? We can become consumed in it, and eventually it overtakes us. And when those issues multiply, we become overwhelmed by it all.

And beneath the surface is another familiar fear: *If I slow down, everything might fall apart. If I don't do it, who will?* But when leaders operate from the need to be needed, they drift outside their role and away from their purpose. Their decisions become bottlenecked, and now teams are stuck waiting. The leader becomes essential to everything and effective at very little. Remember, resist the urge to fix everything. Leading with clarity interrupts that pattern, restores boundaries, names ownership, and reconnects leaders to what is truly theirs to carry. When leaders know who they are, clarity about what to do follows.

On stage was the CEO of one of California's largest healthcare providers. During his keynote, he shared a slide with the following question: "Do you know what one of the leading causes of death in the U.S is today? The answer? Hypertension. Do you know what one of the main contributors is? Chronic stress. Better known as the silent killer because it sneaks up on us, sometimes without any notice. Many of us believe we can handle the stresses of our jobs, that we are immune, or, in many cases, in denial about it. Our bodies learn to mask it, fooling us into thinking all is fine until it's not. Many leaders carry stress as a badge of honor until it quietly becomes a cost.

Maya prided herself on being a high achiever, the kind of business leader who never dropped a ball. After all, she was considered a seasoned manager by her colleagues. One particular day, her calendar was a rainbow of meetings, quarterly reporting, project updates, employee check-ins, crises, and "quick questions." She moved through the company halls like a pinball; fast, responsive, and always in motion. People described her as dependable. She privately described herself as drowning, often feeling stressed and worried she would let her team down.

Most days, Maya bounced from one conversation to the next, solving problems before people even finished explaining them. Her team leaned on her for everything, and she told herself that meant she was doing her job well. But the truth? She no longer felt like she was leading, but rather simply reacting.

One Tuesday morning, three people stopped her before she even reached her office. By 9:00 a.m., her plan for the day was in ashes. That's when her supervisor's words surfaced:

- *What matters most right now?*
- *What's mine to do and what isn't?*
- *Who needs to be part of this decision?*
- *What kind of leader do you want to be?*

Maya shut her door, a radical act for her, and answered honestly. What mattered most was a staffing decision she had been avoiding.

> *What was hers to do was set direction and communicate it clearly.*
> *Who needed to be involved was her project team, not Maya alone.*
> *What kind of leader she wanted to be was one who was collaborative and trustworthy.*

She delegated, scheduled, and gathered the right people. The noise didn't disappear, but it stopped dictating her day. Clarity didn't make the work smaller. It made it manageable and aligned her actions with her role instead of her insecurities. By the end of the day, she was reminded of a truth she had forgotten in her season of striving: When you know who you are, clarity about what to do follows naturally.

The striver in us tells us to do more. To say yes. To keep proving, producing, and pushing forward. And for a while, that pace feels like strength. But over time, that strength can quietly turn on us.

Arthur Brooks (2022) names this dynamic the **striver's curse**, the pattern in which high achievers, like Maya, begin to fear decline, feel less satisfied by their accomplishments, and notice their relationships fraying under the weight of constant pursuit. His research suggests that for many who have built their identity around achievement, success alone eventually stops delivering what it once did. Without a shift, purpose, connection, and joy begin to erode—even as external success continues to grow.

When we operate without clarity, we drift into the Striver's Curse: busy, needed, responsive...but not aligned. And without alignment, every unforeseen challenge pulls us off course, every crisis becomes ours to solve, and every task feels urgent, whether it truly matters or not.

And this is where the shift must begin. Because the Striver isn't struggling from a lack of effort. They are overwhelmed by indecision. Not big decisions, but small ones. What matters most, what can wait, what is mine to carry, and what is not. Without those decisions, everything stays in motion. Everything feels important. And the work never quite moves forward. Our experience has taught us that the turning point doesn't come from doing more. It comes from deciding differently. Because clarity is not about having all the answers. It's about being willing to name what matters most, even when it means letting something else go.

Clarifying Cues

Clarifying changes the equation. Clarifying doesn't arrive all at once. It arrives through intentional questions:

- What are we actually trying to accomplish?
- By when?
- With whom?

Distraction, not difficulty, is the greatest threat to clarity. Skipping this work guarantees that execution will be reactive and misaligned. Clarifying early doesn't slow momentum. It prevents rework.

And clarifying isn't just personal; it must be shared. The work is too complex, and the stakes too high, for leaders to operate alone. When leaders try to carry everything themselves, they become the bottleneck. When they build clarity with others, they create shared ownership, shared responsibility, and better decisions.

When Marcus became principal of a struggling middle school, he fixed everything himself until a colleague said, "When you fix everything, you keep us from leading anything." It stopped him cold. At the next meeting, Marcus came in, not with a plan, but with questions:

- *What has worked in the past?*
- *Who should be on the planning team?*
- *Why does this matter for our students and families?*
- *What would success actually look like?*

Instead of the meeting being led by Marcus and his "plan," the meeting was led by the team to clarify the work ahead and to find the right people to ensure its success. Marcus left with a plan much better than he could have completed by himself, and his team walked away with a deeper sense of shared purpose and excitement for the revisions to an established building event.

Lone wolves work harder. Coalitions work smarter. That shift doesn't happen by accident. It happens when leaders stop saying yes to everything and start leading with clarity. When everything feels important, focus isn't found in doing more, but in deciding what earns your yes—and what requires a boundary:

- Is this mine to lead, or mine to support?
- Does this move our top priority forward?
- Am I the only one who can do this?

If not, pause. Delay it. Delegate it. Or decline it. Not everything is yours to carry. And when everything matters, nothing moves.

Micro Moves for Meaningful Momentum

Simple practices to determine what is yours to carry.

CLARIFY — Focus Before Frenzy
If *Pause* creates space to think, *Clarify* determines what deserves that space. Every act of focus is a decision about who and what matters most.

Guiding Question: *What matters most right now, and what can wait?*

Purpose: Clarify provides an opportunity to translate awareness into direction. Clarify helps leaders move from scattered efforts to aligned priorities.

Prompts: Choose one—clarity requires restraint:
- What is essential, and what is optional?
- If I could move only one thing forward this week, what would it be?
- What am I doing out of habit, guilt, or expectation rather than purpose?
- Who needs to be part of this, and who doesn't?

Outcome: A leader who channels energy toward what matters most: reducing overload, increasing impact, and protecting focus from frenzy.

What This Looks Like In Practice

Leading with intention instead of intensity.

- Naming one priority for the day that, if accomplished, makes the day a win.
- Using a simple filter before saying yes: *Does this align with our goals right now?*
- Ending meetings with: *What's the one thing we need to move forward?*

- A weekly focus check: *What moved the mission, and what just filled the calendar?*

Clarity doesn't eliminate work. It orders it. It replaces the pressure to do everything with permission to do the *right* things well.

Your Next Move

From confusion to confidence.

Clarity turns confusion into confidence. It's what allows leaders to move from reaction to resolution, from activity to alignment. When we clarify our purpose, priorities, and people, we free ourselves and our teams from the fog of overwork.

Stop trying to do everything.
Start focusing on what matters most right now.

When leaders clarify, they create calm. And calm creates trust. Clarity doesn't quiet the work. It amplifies what matters most.

PART IV

ACT...with Purpose

Making Movements, Maintaining Momentum

<table>
<tr><td>PAUSE
...with stillness</td></tr>
<tr><td>CLARIFY
...with focus</td></tr>
<tr><td>ACT
...with Purpose</td></tr>
<tr><td></td></tr>
</table>

How do I move the work forward with others before I feel ready?

The questions leaders often have on their minds.

What if I don't know where to begin?
What if the plan isn't good enough?
What if people don't like it?

The leaders we encounter don't struggle to care. Some struggle to move. Others move, but don't move with intention or where their movements are most needed. For many of our colleagues, their moves feel fragmented rather than moves that build momentum. They often move quickly from one fire to the next, failing to pause and clarify what matters most, leaving them mentally exhausted and unsure what to do next. Eventually, this creates a new dilemma—taking the next step with confidence. Because once you know what matters, standing still becomes a decision, too. And leadership was never meant to be practiced from the sidelines.

Why Action Matters

Why standing still is also a decision.

Leadership tempts us toward control. We tell ourselves: *If we plan long enough, think through every variable, and manage every detail, the outcome will match the vision.* But overplanning rarely produces excellence, especially in isolation. More often than not, it produces a delay.

> ***Act* is the smallest visible step that moves the work forward *by building ownership in others*, without waiting for perfect conditions.**

Leaders often step in, solve it themselves, or keep refining the plan instead of moving the work forward with others. Over time, decisions made in isolation lead to weak implementation because no one else feels responsible for the outcome. Instead, share your first draft and move the work forward with others—even before it feels ready. *Act:* when you stop protecting the plan and start serving the people.

Act: when you stop protecting the plan and start serving the people.

That's exactly where Daryl found himself that summer when he stepped into his new role as a high school principal.

Acting in Action

When progress begins with one imperfect step.

In June, when Daryl became the new high school principal, he was charged with revamping Professional Learning Communities (PLCs) at his high school. During his transition, the superintendent shared with him that although they had been investing in the PLC process for over ten years, they were still not yielding the results she had hoped for. Instead of working as a unified team that focused on student learning, discussions were often dominated by only a few staff members who spoke individually about their experiences with specific students and their families, often looking to the administration for a resolution.

Over the summer, Daryl researched and visited other schools. He connected with other leaders, but he soon found himself in an all too familiar position where we often land in leadership; he was information-rich, implementation-poor. His intentions were noble, but he struggled with where to begin.

By October, the articles were stacked on the corner of his desk like a quiet accusation and each visit to a PLC reminded him they were still stuck in the same old routines: bring a long list of students to talk about, get side-tracked with frustrations about what wasn't working, get through a handful of students, and walk out still worried about all the students they didn't get to. By November, guilt started turning into shame: *Why did they hire me? Why do I keep getting sidetracked? How do I keep the momentum going?*

In that moment, Daryl knew that the longer he waited, the heavier the pressure would feel. So he did one brave thing that wasn't flashy, but it was decisive: He shut his door, set a timer for thirty minutes, and back mapped the next steps:

- What is my vision for what I hope to accomplish?
- What is one small step I can take to get started?
- What progress checks do I want to include in my calendar?

He walked out with a simple timeline and one protected, non-negotiable block each week dedicated to PLC implementation. He also asked for support: a mentor, a sounding board, someone to help him keep moving when the hiccups came. Nothing about that was perfect. But it was responsible. And it was progress.

Purposeful action is responsive, not reckless. It says, *I don't need to be ready. I need to take the next step.* Still, Daryl couldn't help but wonder if it was the correct path to take.

What We Have Learned

Why learning cultures outperform control cultures

In our work with leaders, we've found that progress doesn't accelerate when leaders move faster—it accelerates when they stop carrying the work alone. Research and practice consistently show that learning cultures outperform control cultures because they distribute ownership rather than centralize it.

In a previous book (Casas and Birk, 2024), Jimmy describes the impact of "Layering the Leadership," stating that when leaders act in a purposeful way by slowing down and spending more time layering the process on the front end, leaders will experience greater success not only in making positive change but also in improving morale. When leadership is strategic and intentional, working with all staff members using the layering process, rather than in isolation or with a select few, they are able to see a greater impact–the impact that Daryl was hoping to see. Organizations that practice shared leadership and take time to use their teams strategically, layering them one drop at a time, generate better results by fostering shared ideas, dissenting voices, inviting feedback, acknowledging uncertainty, and reducing negative undercurrents. These environments outperform those driven by control because people feel trusted to contribute and learn as they go.

What often stalls leaders isn't external resistance, but internal narrative. Limiting our mindset about our readiness, capacity, or worthiness can slow action even when clarity is present. Purposeful leadership begins when leaders move anyway, taking small, intentional steps and seeking much-needed support from other team members. Over time, these visible acts do more than create progress. They build systems grounded in vision, clarity, trust, and shared ownership—one small step at a time.

The Controller Archetype

Holding Everything. Trusting Nothing.

Every leader carries a quiet internal voice within them that we call "The Controller." Emily was no exception. The look on her face said it all, even before the words left her mouth: "I'm worried that if I give up control, things won't get done right. I know that I can't do it all, but I am not sure I am ready to let things go."

At a very young age, Emily learned that she was pretty good at teasing out the actionable steps in any given problem or issue, and then she would act. She would solve the problem, fix the broken, heal the wound. All before she'd have to be at the bus stop. She trained herself to look for people and situations and insert herself where she could act. Acting felt good and honest. Acting felt useful. Acting helped to define who she was as a person.

Emily was fueled by action in all areas of her life. Her success in work, family, parenting, and life in general came from the ever-present list of completed steps and tasks. Her entire identity was wrapped up in what she could do, what she could produce. There was no time afforded for planning, let alone reflecting. The proof was in the completion of the task—and there were plenty of tasks to complete.

When she was asked to step into her current role, it was widely known that she was inheriting a role that needed urgent attention. Almost immediately, she was flooded with necessary "actions." Tasks and responsibilities that required speed and urgency—two things that she was particularly adept at. For a solid year, she uncovered issues, made decisions for her teams, and kept the ball rolling. It was exhausting, but she knew the urgency would soon die down and her team members would eventually pick up the slack.

But that never happened. She remained consistently swamped and frustrated. Building and district leaders continued to bring issues to her without attempting to find solutions. Staff would ask her to look into things that had been broken for a long, long time, without resolution. Resentments grew, as did the frustrations. She quickly realized that her exhaustive efforts to clear problems and issues for people had not made one bit of difference in how these people solved their own problems. Instead of imparting problem-solving structures and strategies, she had told them that the only strategy they needed was her.

Emily shared that working with a coach helped her to see that she had been committed to an old, outdated measure of success. Sure, a list of individually completed tasks is nice, but growing her internal leadership structures so others can also be highly productive was priceless. The only way to do that successfully is to pause, asking before you act, what you want to spend your time on—growing your team or checking boxes. It is only through slowing down that Emily realized her efforts will come back to her tenfold if she remembers to focus on the right things before she acts.

This commitment to growing capacity in her leaders is a shift that she must work on daily. She is frequently met with tasks that she could take care of quickly and easily, but then she remembers her refined goal of empowering and growing her team and learning to let go. With that as the focus, she learned to move to the side, supporting rather than doing. It's slow work, but she truly believes this is where she can make the greatest impact, and more importantly, not overmanage others.

Perhaps, like Emily, you find yourself hustling as fast as you can and then sprinting to the finish line, thinking this will give you the best chance to solve the daily dose of problems that exist in your organization. What you may not see, that we hope to bring to light, is that when you act quickly on your own to solve every problem for everyone, you are causing a different type of drip, the type that slowly leads to a quiet dependency. Because doing it right yourself is often the fastest way to ensure your team never learns to do it at all.

In environments of urgency, control, and high expectations, leaders often stall, not because they lack clarity, but because they are reluctant to let go of that first step, a step they feel comfortable taking. Every leader has a Controller within them, the part that wants airtight plans, predictable outcomes, and minimized risk. At first, the logic feels responsible: If I can control enough variables, everything will be fine.

Just one more change.
Just one more data point.
Just one more conversation before I decide.

But leading as a Controller comes with hidden costs:

While you're refining the plan, the team is waiting.
While you're perfecting the message, momentum slows.
While you're trying to eliminate risk, progress quietly stalls.
While you are working alone, people are quietly quitting.

Controllers don't slow leadership because leaders are weak. They slow leadership because they care:

You want the idea to be good.
You want people to believe in the direction.
You want the plan to work.
You want your team to experience success.

Leadership was never meant to operate in isolation or perfect conditions. The longer we wait for certainty and the more control we take on, the heavier leadership becomes. The drips will begin to pour like a faucet. Over-managing doesn't create stability. It magnifies stress, yours and everyone else's.

It is not uncommon for district and building leaders to find themselves in situations similar to those of Jordan described earlier in the *Pause* section, Daryl at the start of this chapter, or even Emily in the story above. We regularly encounter leaders who deal with the emotional labor and stress of having to act alone, overextending themselves, and then having to revisit their decisions when the pushback comes back at them tenfold. We listen to stories in the field from leaders who have encountered moments when they did their best to implement a change, but the change initiative did not yield the intended results.

None of us should judge Daryl for the decision he made the day he shut the door and mapped out his steps. As we learned, his idea to do so was decisive, and it also relieved the pressure that had been building. It also garnered results, but the question is: Did his idea to move quickly in those thirty minutes on his own maximize the impact he was hoping to make? Like Daryl, many leaders often question whether their ideas are good. Rory Sutherland, a behavioral economist and author of *Alchemy: The Surprising Power of Ideas That Don't Make Sense*, states that the opposite of a good idea can also be a good idea (2020). In other words, the conventional, solo path forward may have fared better with more support from others. Daryl walked out with a simple timeline and one protected block each week dedicated to PLC implementation, but now what?

Daryl's intentions to move forward were good, and he believed it would help both teachers and students, but we later learned not to the level he had hoped. The weekly PLC meetings that he had stated would be non-negotiable soon became negotiable, with staff consistently not showing up, and when they did, they often did not contribute anything of value to the meeting. Over time, this created tension among team members when, once again, the same team members found themselves doing most of the heavy lifting while others were allowed to just sit there and be a passenger in life. We often say that the difference between excellent cultures and those that struggle is that excellent cultures do not allow people to opt out.

So, what can we take away from this experience upon reflection? When we move too quickly to solve problems, we create distance between ourselves and the very people we're trying to support. We unintentionally build systems that rely on us instead of strengthening the people within them. That's the hidden cost of control.

Layering change—one step at a time, with others—does more than improve outcomes. It builds ownership. It protects trust. And it ensures the work can continue without you at the center. Because when leadership becomes person-dependent, progress is fragile. But when it becomes process-dependent, progress is sustainable. That shift requires more than awareness. It requires us to act in the moment. And if you find it difficult to make that shift, remember this: Anything that is difficult to do is just an action unrehearsed. When you feel the urge to step in, fix it, or perfect it:

> Anything that is difficult to do is just an action unrehearsed.

- Pause the impulse to take over.
- Name the risk you're trying to avoid. (*What am I afraid will go wrong?*)
- Invite ownership instead of inserting control.
- Take one step back—even if it feels slower.

Then ask: *What would it look like to let someone else carry this—even if it isn't done perfectly?* Because leadership isn't defined by how well you execute. It's defined by how well others grow in your absence.

Layering Systemic Change

Acting with purpose over time.

We know every building includes staff members who could easily be considered superstars. However, what we consistently see is that many of those stars are not aligned. Before moving forward with any new change, we highly recommend taking the following steps to ensure your team is aligned before implementing any next steps:

> **What** – Vision: What is the plan, and what are the expectations associated with it?
>
> **Why** – Purpose: Is the reason for implementing this change clear?
>
> **How** – Voice: Who will be impacted by this change, and whose voices need to be included?

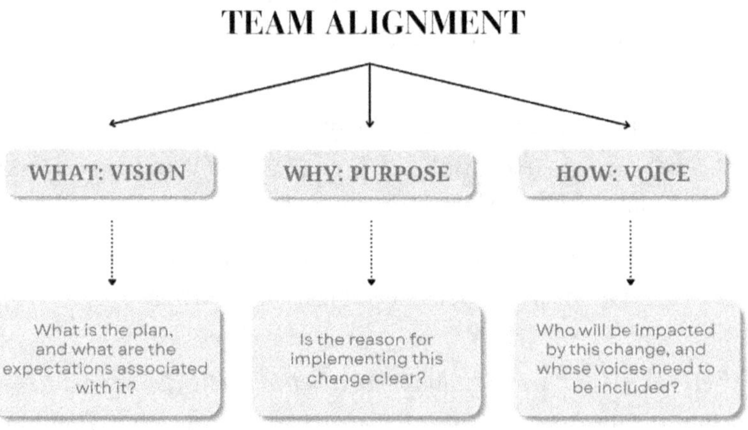

Leaders must be able to clearly articulate what they hope to accomplish and why it matters. When we are not clear from the outset, we leave room for others to create their own narrative about why the change is happening, and that narrative is often negative.

Once the vision and the purpose have been clearly communicated, leaders must intentionally seek input from those most impacted by the change. It is equally important to explain why we are seeking input and how that feedback will be used. At this stage, leaders must clearly communicate what they expect to occur as a result of the change.

When we collect feedback but fail to act on it, we risk losing credibility. People may feel their time has been wasted or, worse, begin to question whether leadership has the courage or capacity to make the improvements needed. The first exposure to any new initiative is critical. Mistakes during the initial launch can quickly push leaders into recovery mode, which is one reason change can feel so exhausting. One common misstep occurs when initiatives are first introduced in large group settings. This approach can create unnecessary complications. Instead, we encourage leaders to be more strategic and intentional. Being strategic means being transparent and honest about the reasoning behind the change and on how we move through the process. Below is how we recommend using the Drip Effect Framework to ensure that we Pause, Clarify, Act, and Refine throughout each layer of the change process.

When we talk about change, it's important to understand that every organization is made up of layers, and each layer is both part of the larger system and a system on its own. In a school district, that includes the central office, the building level, the classroom, and ultimately the students we're trying to impact.

The key is recognizing that these layers aren't isolated. There's a *throughline* that connects them, and how one layer operates directly influences the others. If we want to implement change effectively, we must honor that connection. At its core, a system works when it replicates itself with alignment at every level.

So what does that look like in practice? It starts at the central office level. First, a superintendent pauses to really understand the bigger picture and to clarify their vision prior to making the next move. Once that is clear in their mind, they share that vision with their closest team members, clearly explaining the why behind it, and then do something just as important: invite those team members into the process. *Help me see what I don't see. What challenges could this create? Where might this break down?* That conversation happens within their own layer first. Depending on the size of the school district, this will look different. In larger districts, it might begin with a discussion among cabinet members, assistant superintendents, directors, coordinators, etc. In smaller districts, it may be a business manager and a curriculum specialist or student services coordinator. The key is for a superintendent to identify individuals to serve as that initial layer. This helps slow the process down and work toward clarity and alignment before ever moving forward.

Once that alignment is in place, the work "drips" to the next layer: building leaders. Now, the superintendent brings principals into the conversation: "Here's what we're thinking. Here's why. What are we missing?" One thing we know from our experience is that principals see things from their level that we often miss at the central office level, and we need their help to avoid potential missteps and deep undercurrents that could stall the change process or negatively impact people's attitudes around the change. What we see is that when principals are given a voice to add their perspective early in the initial stages, share their concerns, and help refine the work, they are also learning how to slow down and allow others to take part in the change process. This is crucial for their growth. The goal isn't for the central office to lead change in buildings. The goal is to *teach principals how to lead it themselves so they, in turn, can teach others.* After having it modeled by their superintendent, principals return to their buildings and replicate the same approach. They engage assistant principals, then their leadership teams, and eventually the full staff, pausing each time to see the bigger picture: sharing the vision, clarifying the why, and asking for input. And let's not forget the students who are also a part of the layering and in some cases, may prove to have the most important voices of all. Teachers are more likely to replicate this process in classrooms with their students when it has been modeled, encouraged, and supported by administration

This layered approach has proven more effective in the field than launching an initiative with the entire staff immediately. We recommend beginning with a smaller cohort, like a building teacher leadership team. This smaller group can help design a more strategic process for implementation, allowing the team to work with you through potential challenges and experience early successes. These early connections also build trust and confidence among team members, empowering them to support their colleagues when the process expands to grade-level or departmental teams. Developing the capacity of others is a crucial step in scaffolding change. One thing we know for certain: If a small group of teacher leaders cannot effectively implement a change, it is highly unlikely the entire staff will be able to implement it with fidelity.

What works better in our experience is a slow drip. Layer by layer. Conversation by conversation. Clarity, purpose, and alignment before action. When we follow these steps and take time to debrief as a team afterwards to refine the work, we develop a fresh new mindset, believing that together, we can accomplish anything. The superintendent models each step of the framework with their team, then hands it off to principals. At that point, the process restarts at the building level and flows down to teachers and, ultimately, students. That handoff is critical. It signals trust, builds capacity, and reinforces that principals are responsible for leading change in their buildings. The diagram below illustrates how each district-level layer aligns with a corresponding layer at the building level. When these layers mirror one another, they reinforce and replicate shared practices, creating a cohesive system. When this alignment is absent, the layers operate in isolation rather than as an integrated whole.

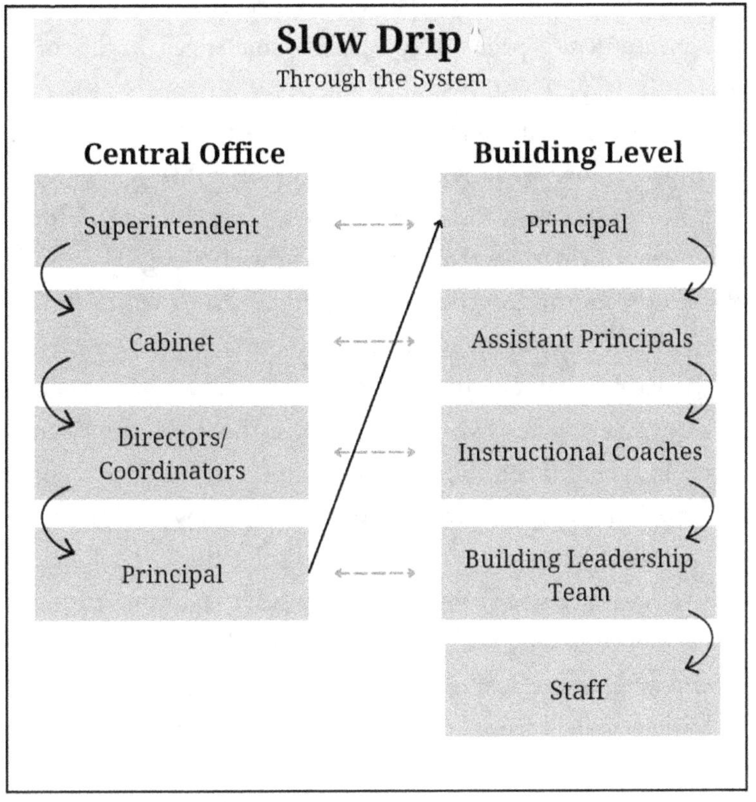

So why do so many leaders and organizations struggle to implement change effectively? Because too often, we move at a sprinter's pace or, in this case, a track athlete's long jump. We try to make a change from the superintendent or central office level straight to the staff. It's a leap that skips the system entirely, and when that happens, alignment breaks down, ownership is lost, and implementation suffers. So, the next question is, "Why do leaders leap rather than layer?" The most common response: *"We simply don't have time for this."* But perhaps the better question is: How would we prefer to spend our time? Working collaboratively with fellow leaders, educators, students, and the community to proactively identify challenges, brainstorm ideas, prototype solutions, and reflect on outcomes tends to be the work that fills our buckets as educational leaders. Yes, this approach may require front-end investment (e.g., planning time, a few meetings, and several hours along the way). However, with more perspectives examining the challenge and more collective brainpower working toward solutions, the likelihood of identifying a human-centered solution that works for everyone increases significantly.

Conversely, when we fail to involve those who will ultimately implement the solution, the chances of creating a positive experience are low. Even more concerning, we fail to build the capacity within our community to solve future challenges. In those situations, we often end up spending far more time on the back end dealing with confusion, complaints, resentment, and the inevitable question: "Why didn't you just ask us?"

Whether it is front-end time or back-end time, it is still time. The difference is that the front end is far more productive and immeasurably more pleasant. By slowing down and intentionally layering the process on the front end, we believe leaders will experience greater success not only in implementing positive change but also in improving staff morale.

When leadership is strategic and intentional, working with staff rather than in isolation, the impact is greater at each level. When the layers in an organization model and replicate the same process, you don't just have an initiative, you have a system. And systems, when done well, no longer have to rely on chance. They build clarity, communicate effectively, create consistency, and significantly increase the likelihood that when leaders follow a framework, change actually sticks and, more importantly, positive results are achieved.

Act Cues

How to know if you're acting—or controlling.

Here's a truth many leaders won't readily admit: We don't always feel confident. Not because we doubt our calling, but because leadership puts us in situations where the outcome is never certain. Quiet confidence isn't loud. It's steady. And sometimes our hesitation isn't about clarity; it's about control. When the next move isn't obvious, we default to what feels safest: holding on, stepping in, or doing it ourselves. If you're stuck, ask yourself:

> Anything that is difficult to do is just an action unrehearsed.

1. **Who is carrying the work right now?**
   Am I building ownership—or keeping it?
2. **What am I trying to protect?**
   Am I avoiding risk—or avoiding discomfort?
3. **What would it look like to take one step back instead of forward?**
   Where can I invite ownership instead of inserting myself?

And one more filter that matters: If the action isn't meaningful, manageable, and sustainable, it's not an *Act* move; it's a control reflex.

Micro Moves for Meaningful Momentum

Simple practices to start moving with intention and stop moving impulsively.

ACT — with Purpose

Guiding Question: *What is one thing I can release without losing direction?*

Purpose: Action isn't just about movement. It's about making intentional moves that are inspired by clarity and the pause that transforms movement into momentum.

Prompts: Choose one.
+ Send the draft without one more rewrite.
+ Delegate the decision and don't "fix" it later.
+ Pilot the idea with one class, team, or meeting.
+ Ask for input and accept the first viable solution.
+ Name progress publicly before outcomes are known.

Outcome: Leaders create momentum when they act before everything is perfect.

What This Looks Like in Practice

Small moves. Visible courage. Momentum that builds.

- A principal gives feedback after a walkthrough the same day, not weeks later, even if the language isn't perfect.
- A leadership team pilots a new schedule with one grade level instead of waiting for full staff consensus.
- A teacher tries a new strategy mid-unit, gathers quick student feedback, and adjusts in real time.
- A leader delegates a decision fully—and resists the urge to step back in when it feels uncomfortable.
- A difficult conversation happens sooner, with care and clarity, instead of being delayed until it becomes heavier.
- A team names what's working publicly, even before results are finalized, reinforcing progress over perfection.

These are not grand gestures. They are small, visible acts of courage. And over time, they do something powerful: They shift a culture, moving from hesitation to momentum.

Your Next Move

Where purpose meets clarity.

Action is where courage meets clarity. Without it, even the best ideas stay theoretical. When leaders move with intention, they build momentum that energizes teams and keeps vision alive. Acting doesn't mean doing

> For some leaders, the bravest move is releasing control, on purpose, in small ways, every day.
> ———

everything. For some leaders, the bravest move is releasing control, on purpose, in small ways, every day. When we practice courageous action, we:

- Replace control with capacity
- Turn clarity into shared ownership
- Build a culture where progress, not perfection, defines success.

Why purpose sustains momentum.
Perfection stalls. Courage starts. Leaders often stall waiting for ideal conditions, full consensus, or the perfect plan. But progress grows from *doing,* not polishing. When you move with intention, you model learning, invite collaboration, and build the team's collective confidence. If releasing control creates learning, not harm, it counts as success.

Stop overthinking and waiting for certainty.
Start moving forward with others with purpose.

Momentum builds from movement, but it multiples from purposeful movement.

PART V

Refine...with Growth

Learn, Adjust, and Strengthen.
Earn Your Revisions

PAUSE ...with stillness
CLARIFY ...with focus
ACT ...with Purpose
REFINE ...with Growth

How do you know you're getting better if you never look back?

In schools, the temptation is to move on quickly, to chase the next idea, the next goal, the next "fix." But when reflection is skipped, learning is sacrificed. Learning should drive us. As leaders, sometimes we fail to take time to reflect on the impact of our action or plans, and instead quickly pivot to the next task that needs to be accomplished. We also frequently observe this pattern in classrooms. Teachers pose a question, wait a beat, then answer it themselves and move on. Students lose the chance to process, learning gets rushed, and students "hide" because the teacher moves on without a clear understanding of whether students understand the content. When this pattern exists in classrooms, outcomes become diluted.

> *Refine* is reflection in motion, the rhythm that turns experience into wisdom and effort into evolution.

Leadership does the same thing. When we move forward without reflecting, we stay busy and tired, but we don't actually grow. And yes, just like students, teachers also "hide" because we move on too quickly without knowing if the teacher truly grasped what we were trying to do.

Why Refinement Matters

This is where The Drip Effect keeps us on course, and refining is one step that helps us conquer those unhelpful Archetypes that we are all susceptible to grasping onto when we are in the hustle.

The trap for leaders is when we skip reflection because the current system rewards speed. The next task, the next initiative, the next crisis pulls us forward before we've absorbed anything from the last. When leaders treat everything as urgent, nothing gets examined. We stay in motion, but we don't actually move forward. This is the discipline of first things first. Not doing more, but deciding better.

Refinement in Action

It was week two of the new semester, and everything felt uncertain. Hallway transitions were off, staff members were frustrated, and students were testing boundaries. Tony, a first-year principal, wanted to address all the problems immediately. His instinct was to tighten control: create a new plan, call an emergency meeting, initiate hall sweeps—all responses that we have seen on our campus visits that were implemented and ultimately failed—or at least failed to sustain over long periods of time.

But he stopped.

Instead of reacting, he gathered his leadership team and started a reflection process with: *"Let's learn before we change."* They spent time gathering feedback, naming what was working and what wasn't. Then, instead of redoing the whole plan, they adjusted one small routine and communicated it clearly to staff. By the following week, the energy had shifted. People hadn't needed a quick response; they had needed a thoughtful response. When reflection is skipped, insight is lost. And without insight, improvement stalls. *Refine* asks us to stop pressing and start understanding. Reflection isn't retreat. It's recalibration.

What We Have Learned

Why reflection is what makes change stick.

Most change efforts don't fail because the idea was wrong. As we learned in the last chapter, they often fail because the process for implementing the change was ineffective. When leaders move too fast, the process moves fast, and critical steps are missed. And a poor process is often a magnet for a poor result. Organizational leaders are often expected to introduce new systems, initiatives, or strategies, but unless people are given time to discuss, refine, revisit, and internalize them, the change rarely sustains or delivers the desired results. Over time, Tony learned to become a student of the improvement game. He learned it takes practice. He learned that sometimes you have to step on the rake to learn what not to do. And he learned that improvement isn't built through dramatic overhauls; it is built through small adjustments practiced consistently over time.

Reflection plays a critical role in that process. When leaders pause long enough to examine what they've implemented, and ask those who were impacted by the change, what worked, what didn't, and what needs to shift, they turn experience into learning. Structured reflection, using clear prompts, brief timeframes, and consistent routines, significantly accelerates skill development compared to simply repeating the same actions without reflection. In other words, learning does not come from activity alone. It comes from examining the activity.

In today's leadership environment, the pace of work continues to accelerate. Leaders are expected to respond quickly, solve problems in real time, and keep things moving. Over time, this creates a shift toward *doing* over *thinking*, leaving little space for reflection and contributing to what researchers describe as a "shrinking of time"—a constant pressure to do more, faster, with less opportunity to process experience (van der Steen et al., 2021).

Psychological safety also strengthens refinement. When leaders invite reflection through open conversation and peer feedback, they create a culture in which blind spots are more easily seen, and enhancing the culture becomes not only a shared responsibility among a few people, but also sends a clear message that cultivating a healthy culture is everyone's responsibility. Over time, change is influenced through these small learning loops when they are compounded. Leaders notice the patterns sooner, allowing their teams to adjust more quickly. These practices soon become habits, and healthy habits lead to healthy change, and, eventually, a healthier culture.

We've all been there. We walk into the day with a clear plan, and then it happens:

The urgent phone call.
A lack of sub coverage.
A student altercation.
A situation that suddenly needs your attention now.

By midday, our best intentions are buried under the belief that everything matters. That belief is what breaks refinement. This was the case with Breanna.

The board vote was 6–0. Breanna still recalls the rush of adrenaline and the pride she felt hearing the board member announce her as the new Assistant Superintendent for one of the best districts in Alabama. After twenty years of giving it her all, it felt like she had finally reached the mountaintop.

But here's what no one tells you about climbing the ladder: the higher you go, the thinner the air becomes. Some days, it's hard to breathe. Admittedly, the transition has been a struggle for Breanna. Instead of feeling like a "boss," she's wrestled with a persistent, uninvited thought that follows her throughout most days—the feeling that she's not enough. Her inner critic doesn't whisper. It shouts.

In a profession obsessed with being everything to everyone and where everything matters, we're expected to have all the answers, ask the right questions, and carry ourselves with certainty from the moment we're handed the keys to the office. But this past year hasn't brought Breanna clarity or confident, decisive moves. Instead, she has felt anxious and emotionally drained. She hesitates, worried about making the wrong decision. At times, she feels unprepared for the task at hand. She's even shed a few tears. Some days, the weight of it all makes her want to shout, "Get me out of here!" It's exhausting to feel like you're dropping the ball on a dream you spent twenty years chasing.

Recently, though, she's found herself reflecting on her current reality, and her perspective has shifted. She's come to realize that feeling like she's not enough isn't a sign of weakness. It's a sign of stewardship. If she didn't care deeply about the thousands of students and teachers counting on her, she wouldn't feel the weight of the role or the gravity of daily decisions. That sense of inadequacy exists because she understands what's at stake. She cares too much about doing right by her staff, students, and families to offer anything less than her best. That isn't failure; it's integrity.

Lately, we've watched her become more intentional, slowing down, focusing on what she can control, and approaching each day with purpose. She's more mindful in her interactions and more deliberate in her actions, ensuring that what she does truly matters. This shift has strengthened how she regulates her emotions and her response to challenges.

She knows she can't do everything or fix every problem—that's a trap she refuses to fall into. Rather, she's re-examined where she needs to put her energy. By refining her True North: connecting and collaborating with people, slowing down to think and understand before responding, and keeping the main thing the main thing—which is, and always has been, the kids and her teachers.

For Breanna, she struggled to identify where and when her energy was needed the most. Reflection required space, and space required choice. Leaders who feel responsible for everything end up refining nothing. Refinement asks a harder question than *What needs attention?* It asks: *What deserves attention right now?* This is the discipline of first things first. Not doing more, but deciding better. Choosing what gets focus, what gets deferred, and what no longer earns energy. When we stop chasing productivity and start honoring priority, something shifts. When Breanna finally decided to shift, she didn't lose momentum. She regained her purpose.

Organizations can introduce a dozen new systems, initiatives, or strategies, but unless people have time to refine, repeat, and internalize them, nothing truly changes. We don't grow by doing more. We grow by learning from what we've done. A new initiative launches. Energy is high. The language sounds right. And then, before the work has time to take root, we're already chasing the next improvement. Nothing sticks because nothing is refined.

Refinement is the step we skip when urgency replaces learning. It's the discipline of slowing down just enough to ask: *What's actually working? What needs to be adjusted? What's worth keeping?* Here's a simple way to understand why refinement matters. The red car theory reminds us that if you decide to buy a red car, you suddenly start seeing red cars everywhere. They didn't multiply. Your attention recalibrated. Once your brain is cued to notice something, it finds it. Leadership works the same way. What leaders focus on shows up. What they ignore quietly repeats.

Refinement sharpens attention. It helps leaders notice patterns before they become problems and recognize progress before it gets overlooked. It turns reflection into a leadership habit, not an afterthought. And that's how change becomes culture. Not through announcements. Not through binders or slogans. But through behaviors that are practiced, adjusted, and reinforced until they feel normal. Refinement doesn't slow the work. It strengthens it.

Through intentional reflection and small adjustments, we can turn effort into effectiveness and ideas into habits. New practices stop feeling new and start feeling more like "how we do things around here."

The Dreamer Archetype

Inspired. Imaginative. Inconsistent.

Elena had a reputation. Not for being disorganized or unprepared, but for having *ideas*. Lots of them.

Her team used to joke that you didn't walk into a meeting with her without two things: coffee and extra sticky notes. Because at any moment, she might start sketching something out. A new advisory model, a fresh take on family engagement, even a full rebrand for the school. And the thing was...they were good. Really good. You could feel it when you left her office. That sense that something important was just about to happen. Inspiration was never the issue. It was everything that came after.

Last fall, she rolled out a strategic plan at the all-staff meeting. It was thoughtful, bold, exactly what she thought the school needed. Heads were nodding. People were writing things down. There was real belief in the room, not just in the plan, but in her. And then...nothing. Not all at once. Just slowly.

By November, the energy had worn off. Not because the plan missed the mark, but because no one quite knew what to do next. Questions started piling up, and timelines got fuzzy. A few people tried to move things forward, but most just waited, hoping for a little more clarity that never quite came.

Meanwhile, Elena, who had a propensity for moving quickly, had already moved on to the next idea. Now it was community partnerships. And underneath it all, a quiet, familiar loop kept running in her head: Why is this so easy for me to see but so hard to move forward? How do other leaders actually get things done? Why do I keep starting...and not finishing?

This wasn't about discipline. It wasn't about effort. It was about rhythm. Because when your strength is vision, it's easy to live in that space, where ideas come quickly and feel almost complete the moment they take shape. But without the time (and structure) to slow down, to pressure-test, to revisit, to refine…they never quite land. They stay ideas. And that's the tension.

The Dreamer brings the vision. But without traction, even the best ideas don't go very far. Before progress can take hold, perspective has to come first.

Like Elena, Marquita's first thought came fast and unfiltered: *I am not doing this well enough.* The feedback itself wasn't harsh. In fact, much of it was affirming. Failure rates were down, attendance data was stabilizing, and more importantly, relationships were strengthening. In only her second year as principal of the Career Tech center, she had made steady progress in her goal areas. Still, the moment Marquita finished reading her mid-year evaluation, her attention locked onto the gaps, the places where more focus, more consistency, more refinement were needed.

That is where her thinking zoomed in. She replayed sentences, magnified critiques, overlooked context, and ignored progress. Nothing else mattered: not the gains, not the momentum, not the evidence that the work was moving in the right direction. Marquita's inner narrative reduced a complex picture into a single, discouraging conclusion: *I should be further along by now.*

Zooming out tells a different story. Before reacting, Marquita reached out to her leadership coach for a quick check-in. After reading the evaluation, they offered a simple, but clarifying, assignment, one designed to interrupt rumination and invite refinement instead:

- Identify **7–10 things that are going well** based on the evaluation.

- Name **2–3 specific micro-moves** that would strengthen the work.
- Clarify **how progress would be measured**, and what data would signal improvement.

That exercise forced a shift. It widened the lens. When Marquita took the time to zoom out, patterns emerged that she couldn't see before. What she failed to recognize was that most of the work was actually moving forward. The challenges weren't failures–they were signals. Her path forward didn't require a reset after all. It just needed refinement. In our daily work in schools today, too often we see similar patterns emerge. Teachers and leaders focused on the one dark spot rather than all the white space around it. As we were writing this chapter, we reflected on our own experiences, expressing our own regrets of having done the same thing too many times throughout our careers, a glaring reminder of how we can all quickly fall into that negative space. The following story (2017) is a reminder of why it is so important that we do our best to see things differently, to reframe our thinking:

One day, a professor walked into his classroom and announced a surprise test. The students sat anxiously at their desks as he passed out the papers, face down.

Once everyone had a copy, he told them to turn the page and begin. To their surprise, there were no questions—only a single black dot in the center of an otherwise blank page. Noticing their confusion, the professor said, "I want you to write about what you see."

The students, puzzled but obedient, began writing.

At the end of the class, the professor collected the papers and read the responses aloud. Every student, without exception, had described the black dot—its size, its position, its meaning. When he finished reading, the room fell silent.

Then the professor spoke.

"I'm not going to grade this test. I just wanted to give you something to think about. No one wrote about the white space on the page. Everyone focused on the black dot—and that's exactly what we do in our lives."

"We all have a white page to enjoy, but we spend our time fixating on the dark spots. Life is a precious gift, full of reasons to celebrate. It's constantly changing and renewing—through our friends, our work, our love, our families, and the small miracles we experience every day."

"And yet, we insist on focusing on the dark spots: health problems, money worries, what we lack, relationship struggles, family conflicts, and disappointments with others."

"The dark spots are small and few, but we allow them to dominate our thoughts and cloud our happiness."

"Take your eyes off the black dots in your life. Appreciate your blessings. Savor each moment life gives you."

- **Perspective Shift:** The activity encourages consciously moving focus away from problems (the dot) and acknowledging blessings or opportunities (the white space).
- **The "Big Picture" vs. Small Problems:** In work and life, we often focus on one small negative thing (the dot) rather than the, say, 99% of things that are going well.
- **Application in Leadership:** For leaders and teachers, it serves as a reminder to focus on positive behaviors

and growth, rather than fixating on minor, negative, or disruptive actions.

- **Mindfulness:** It serves as a reminder that we choose what we focus our attention on and, consequently, our emotional state.

Throughout the day, thousands of thoughts quickly flash through our minds. When our thinking narrows, and we focus on the black dot, so does our leadership. Fatigue, pressure, and self-doubt have a way of pulling our focus toward what's missing instead of what's moving. That's what Marquita experienced. Zooming out didn't ignore the feedback. It contextualized it. And that distinction matters. Because reflection is not the same as rumination.

Refinement Cues

Refinement turns ideas into impact. The loop is a tool to help Dreamer Archetypes refine their focus. At the end of a cycle—project, plan, week, or initiative—pause and ask:

- **What worked?** (*Name the progress—don't skip this.*)
- **What didn't land?** (*Without judgment.*)
- *What's one adjustment that would make this stronger?*

Then:

- **Capture the learning**
- **Apply it immediately to the next step**

Not later. Not eventually. Because ideas don't gain traction through inspiration. They gain traction through iteration. Reflection is what makes that iteration possible—but not all reflection leads to growth.

"Well, I guess I'm just not very good at this."

For many educators, this is where minds wander after an evaluation or a complex conversation. You walk into the meeting believing most things are going well. The school is moving forward. Your colleagues are working hard. Students are making progress.

But somewhere in the conversation, your spidey-senses tell you that two pieces of feedback don't land the way you intended them to land. And suddenly, those two comments become the entire story. You leave the meeting replaying the moment in your mind. *Why did I say that? They probably think I handled that poorly. Maybe I'm not as effective as I thought.*

Hours later, the loop is still running. That's not reflection. *That's rumination.* Rumination traps leaders in a narrow loop, replaying what went wrong without gaining insight. The emotion grows louder while the insight shrinks. The more energy we spend criticizing ourselves, the less capacity we have to actually improve. The more mental space consumed by self-blame and regret, the less capacity remains for adaptive action.

Reflection, by contrast, creates distance. It allows leaders to observe their thinking rather than be consumed by it. When leaders pause long enough to step back from the emotion of the moment, something important happens. The noise in our heads begins to quiet. Perspective returns. We stop reacting to the feedback and start learning from it.

We've thought about this as zooming in and zooming out.

Both are necessary. But without the ability to move between them, leaders stay stuck, either overwhelmed by detail or detached from reality. Refinement lives in the movement between these two views.

Zoom In → Examine the feedback.
What specifically didn't land? What evidence supports the concern? What part of this feedback might actually help me grow?

Zoom Out → Reclaim the full picture.
What is going well? What progress has been made? How does this moment fit into the broader work of leading this school?

Adjust → Make the next small move.

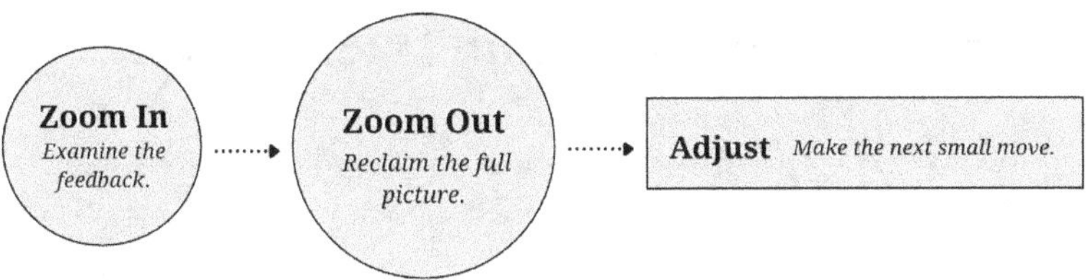

When we zoom in, we examine the data, the feedback, the moments that didn't land the way we hoped. When we zoom out, we regain proportion. We see progress alongside problems. Harsh conclusions turn into informed adjustments for us, helping keep our minds fresh and clear. That's how reflection rebuilds confidence, not through reassurance, but through clarity.

By the time Marquita revisited that evaluation with a more reflective lens, the work ahead felt different. The feedback that once felt heavy now felt specific. Manageable. Actionable. The next steps were smaller. Clearer. Grounded in evidence rather than emotion. She wasn't leading from defensiveness or urgency. She was leading from a lens of learning. And that's what refinement makes possible. Not perfection, but perspective.

Pete Hall, an award-winning principal and author of several books, stated on *The Principal Matters Podcast*, hosted by William Parker (2020), that experience is not always the best teacher. Rather, reflection on experience is the best teacher. By slowing down and reflecting on the experience, we can take away several new learnings that can help us in moving forward, knowing that leaders will continue to find themselves in high-pressure situations where they believe they must act quickly to overcome that feeling.

Micro Moves for Meaningful Momentum

REFINE — *Learn, Adjust, and Strengthen*

Refinement doesn't happen accidentally. It happens through small, intentional practices built into the rhythm of leadership.

Guiding Question: *What did we learn, and what needs to shift next?*

Purpose: Refine transforms experience into growth. It helps leaders move from reflection to adjustment—ensuring that effort leads to improvement, not just repetition.

Prompts: Choose one—growth requires reflection:
- What worked—and why?
- What didn't land—and what can we learn from it?
- What is one adjustment that would make this stronger next time?
- Where am I reacting instead of learning?
- What is this experience trying to teach me?

Core Practices:

Schedule reflection.
End units, events, projects, or grading periods with a brief debrief: What worked? What didn't? What's next?

Use data as dialogue.
Don't treat metrics as verdicts. Ask what they're trying to teach you.

Model humility.
Share what you learned, especially what didn't land. And give others permission to examine their practice without fear.

Create learning loops.
Build small cycles of quick wins → lessons learned → next steps into team time and leadership meetings.

Daily Practices

End the day with a two-minute reflection: *What worked? What didn't?*

What surprised me?

Ask one person for real feedback: *"How did I show up today?"*

Adjust one thing tomorrow based on what today taught you.

Look at data as dialogue: *What stories sit beneath the numbers?*

Capture a "keep, stop, start" list every Friday.

Outcome: A leader who earns their revisions—learning, adjusting, and strengthening both their practice and the system over time.

What This Looks Like in Practice

Refinement keeps us agile, grounded, and aligned with what matters most. It turns mistakes into mentors, experiments into evolution, and routines into systems that actually serve our students, staff, and the entire school community. We don't grow by doing more. We grow by learning from what we've done.

Stop chasing perfection.
Start learning through revision.

What many leaders don't realize is this: reflection doesn't stay personal; it becomes visible. It shapes how you show up-and over time, how your systems function. Leadership doesn't operate in isolation. It echoes:

> We don't grow by doing more. We grow by learning from what we've done.

In every meeting you lead. In every decision you make. In every moment, you either rush… or remain present.

Whether you realize it or not, your pace becomes the pace of the people around you. One leader reflected in the parking lot at the end of the day. Early in her tenure, she noticed the number of cars still there when she was leaving, long after she needed to be. One night, she asked one of her staff members, "Why are you still here?"

The response: *"Because you are."*

Our presence sets a signal. Not just for what gets done, but for how the work gets done. Hustle Culture taught us we don't stop until the work is done. The Drip Effect reminds us: the work will always be there—but how we show up determines whether it is done well. When a leader operates in constant urgency, the system follows. Conversations shorten. Decisions speed up. People *react* instead of *reflect*.

Even well-intended moments can become distractions and fragment the day. What feels like accessibility can quietly become disruption. Priorities shift. Focus splinters. And in an attempt to serve, leaders sacrifice the very work that moves the organization forward.

When a leader shifts, the system shifts.
Not all at once.
Not dramatically.
But consistently.
Drop by drop.

By doing so, we learn that refinement isn't polishing, it's progressing—with wisdom. And when we don't rush wisdom, we earn our revisions.

Your Next Move

Why courage sustains adjustment.

Chasing perfection stalls progress. Reflection moves it forward. Leaders often hesitate to adjust because it requires admitting something didn't work. But growth doesn't come from getting it right the first time. It comes from learning and responding with intention. When you reflect honestly, you model humility, invite feedback, and strengthen your team's collective confidence. If adjusting your approach creates learning, rather than harm, it counts as progress.

PART VI

Becoming a Drip Effect Leader

Small Actions + Steady Pace = Lasting Impact

<table>
<tr><td>PAUSE
...with stillness</td></tr>
<tr><td>CLARIFY
...with focus</td></tr>
<tr><td>ACT
...with Purpose</td></tr>
<tr><td>REFINE
...with Growth</td></tr>
</table>

How do you sustain the ripple?

s this book comes to a close, one truth remains:

You don't have to lead fast to lead well.

The hustle is expensive. Every leader we have encountered in our careers has paid a price, including the two of us. We are no exception. If these pages resonated with you, it's likely because you also have felt the strain of the hustle that was once temporary, likely hidden—but quietly became the norm. But it also came with a cost. The late nights. The constant urgency. The pressure to be everywhere, solve everything, and keep moving, no matter how tired you felt. For many leaders, the sprint was never meant to be permanent. But over time, the sprint became the strategy.

The Drip Effect offers a different way of leading. At the heart of this work is a simple truth:

Small Actions + Steady Pace = Lasting Impact.

Remember Meg from the introduction?

Motion had become her normal, moving quickly, checking boxes, pushing forward. But somewhere along the way, the meaning behind the work began to fade. She was still producing. Still leading. Still achieving. But she was no longer feeling it. Slowing down didn't feel like an option. In fact, it scared her.

For years, her path had been defined by relentless hustle. High expectations, fierce competitiveness, and an unyielding commitment to do more had fueled her rise. By the time she stepped into her dream job as a high school principal, her trajectory seemed unstoppable. But that was also the moment the dam broke.

The pace she had normalized was no longer sustainable. The weight of personal and professional demands became too heavy to carry. She was beyond empty, yet somehow still unable to stop. Always in motion, but with nothing left to give herself.

Part of the struggle was internal. She knew she couldn't keep going like this, but she was scared to let things go. Scared to slow down. Scared of what others might think. Scared to rely on others. She had always been the one people counted on. Asking for help didn't come naturally. And truthfully, she had never felt this kind of helplessness before.

So she avoided. She functioned. She kept moving.

Until she couldn't.

When she finally reached out, it wasn't because she wanted to. It was because she had no other choice. That moment became a turning point. She surrounded herself with people who reminded her that her worth wasn't tied to her performance, and the weight of responsibility is real, and carrying it alone will eventually crush you.

Protecting her peace became essential. And to do that, she had to be intentional. It wasn't anything dramatic—it was small, consistent rituals. Pausing to breathe. Journaling. A short walk between meetings. Creating clearer boundaries between work and home. Even simple acts, like washing off her makeup at the end of the day, changing into comfortable clothes, and intentionally stepping into "mom mode" helped her reset and show up more fully where she was.

She also recognized how her pace had changed her. When she rushed from fire to fire, she lost the humanity and compassion that once defined her leadership. Someone once told her, "It's really hard to be nice when you're in a hurry." That stopped her cold. It forced her to reflect and refine her purpose.

Like all of us, Meg is still a work in progress. But these few intentional shifts have made a profound difference. She makes space for quiet. For joy. For presence. Because she now understands that the hustle was never the answer. In fact, the message is much simpler. Who you surround yourself with matters more than you think, and who you are and what you do matter even more, because it is these moments that recharge the heart that leads.

If you've lost your spark…if you're tired…if you're starting to question your passion…

You are not alone.

Pause. Move with intention. Seek out a community. Ask for help. Small acts. Micro moves. Growth often begins in the most uncomfortable places, but on the other side, there is something better waiting: peace, clarity, purpose, and a renewed sense of who you are meant to be. Consider these suggestions shared by Meg that got her back on track.

When leaders *pause* before pushing through, they model the difference between acting with intention and reacting under pressure. When leaders *clarify* what matters most, they align their efforts with purpose rather than pressure. When they *act* with courage instead of control, progress replaces perfection. And when they *refine* their work over time, learning replaces burnout.

Practiced daily, these rhythms create a ripple effect. You don't have to do everything. You have to do what is connected to your purpose, and do it with consistency. Leadership isn't proven by how many problems you solve. It's proven by how many leaders you build. Along the way, many leaders discover

MICRO MOVES

Remove notifications from phone & watch	Step outside at least once a day
Say "No" to one request today	Slow your walk to a meeting
Create a hard stop at the end of the day	Change clothes when you get home
Protect your peace - home to work	Limit rehashing - take action or let it go

Credit: Meg Simon, 2026

that the beliefs that once fueled their pace begin to change, just like they did for Meg.

The voice that once said: *Slowing down will make me ineffective* is replaced with: *A sustainable pace provides the consistency my team needs.*

The voice that whispered: *I'm letting people down* becomes: *I'm lifting others up to lead well.*

And the fear that warned: *If I pause, things will fall apart* is replaced with a new understanding: *Pausing allows me to think clearly before I act.*

Leadership that lasts isn't built on intensity. It's built on intention.

What Drip Effect Leaders Do Differently

One principal we have known for many years described a leadership challenge that is all too familiar:

Attendance and tardiness in his building were rising. Teachers were frustrated. Data were trending in the wrong direction. Everyone felt pressure to act quickly. The temptation was to react with new rules, new consequences, and new expectations. But instead, this principal chose a different rhythm.

First, he **paused**. Instead of launching a new initiative, he slowed down long enough to understand the problem.

Then he **clarified**. For several days, students who arrived late to class or school completed a short reflection explaining what was happening in their mornings. Patterns quickly began to emerge.

Next, he **acted**. Data revealed that only a small group of students was responsible for most of the tardies. Instead of a school-wide crackdown, the team implemented targeted supports personally designed to reconnect those students with staff and school.

Finally, they **refined** the approach. The interventions were revisited regularly, adjusted when needed, and strengthened over time.

Progress didn't come from perfection. It came from acting on what they actually learned. *The Drip Effect* didn't remove the pressure of leadership, but it did slow him down just enough to give him a rhythm strong enough to respond with clarity instead of urgency. Small actions plus a steady pace equals lasting impact.

What Changes in Practice?

When leaders begin to lead with the *Drip Effect,* the difference is not found in grand gestures. It shows up in the everyday moments that most people overlook.

Meetings begin to feel different.

Hustle culture tells us to go, go, go, and talk, talk, talk. The *Drip Effect* pushes us to do something different: to slow down, to be silent. Too often, leaders are so focused on checking off tasks they don't create time for individual reflection and group conversation. Instead, in their haste, they do the thinking and the work for the team. But when they step back, something shifts. People begin to step forward. Others still won't, but rather than judge, you will be more curious, and slow down to learn why. Insight deepens. Ownership grows. And the work becomes shared, not assigned. Don't be the first to offer help, to give the idea, to be "on." Instead, be present, pause, clarify others' ideas so that actions and refinement become collaborative, rather than emanating from just one voice.

Fleming et al. (2024) found that when psychological safety is low, staff not only perceive their environment more negatively but also experience lower overall well-being. For leaders, the implication is clear: culture cannot be left to chance. It must be built intentionally through consistent efforts to create connected, inclusive environments where people feel safe to engage, contribute, and take professional risks without fear of negative consequences. When that safety is present, people speak more honestly because they are not being hurried toward an answer.

Decisions become clearer.

Not because the work is easier, but because there is greater focus on what actually matters. In increasingly complex, ambiguous environments, the pressure to move quickly can lead leaders to solve everything at once. But when leaders operate with intention, they begin to distinguish between what is urgent and what is essential. They stop trying to solve every problem and start solving the right ones. And in doing so, the work becomes not only more focused but more meaningful.

Conversations go deeper.

When leaders are fully present, they start to notice more things, and people start to feel it. And over time, this noticing has a ripple effect. The team opens up, shares, offers advice, and trusts you and the team more. The Drip Effect gives you permission to stop being on and start focusing on the importance of leaning into others and observing what they need.

Ownership begins to spread.

Because when leaders stop controlling every outcome, others begin stepping into responsibility. Not out of obligation, but because they feel valued and capable. And as this shift happens, trust grows, voices become louder, and outcomes are impacted and owned by the organization, not just the leader.

This is how culture shifts. Not through a new initiative, not through a new expectation. But through a different way of showing up.

How You Lead Is How You Live

Many leaders we spoke to when writing this book acknowledged that maintaining their current pace is not only unsustainable, but also unhealthy. They weren't afraid to admit they felt obligated to take on more work out of a sense of guilt. And that sense of guilt and obligation is what caused them to ignore their own well-being. They believed, *"If I take care of myself, I'm taking away from the people I serve."* But the healthiest leaders eventually discover the opposite is true: taking care of yourself doesn't weaken your leadership, it sustains it.

Personal wellness struggles begin to mount when you lose focus. Your leadership is not just about what you accomplish. It is about the person you are becoming in the process. Not the always-available version. Not the constantly-performing version. The real version. The one who is present enough to notice what matters. Serving others and honoring your own growth are not competing goals. They are connected rhythms. In fact, the moments when leaders slow down often become the moments people remember most.

In *Die with Zero*, Economist Bill Perkins (2020) describes these moments as "memory dividends": the lasting return created when we invest intentionally in meaningful experiences with others. In leadership, those moments matter most early on with students, staff, and colleagues because they show up later as dividends in the form of trust, relationships, and cultures long after the moment itself has passed.

When we slow down, stay in conversations longer, ask better questions, listen more than talk, collaborate more, and show up in classrooms and team meetings, we're not just filling time. We're building trust. Creating these shared experiences is not difficult; rather, it is just unrehearsed. These simple acts, when compounded over time, strengthen relationships and shape cultures that endure long after we've moved on. Sometimes the simple and uncomplicated is the best path to take. Move too fast, and the dividends disappear. When we intentionally and consistently slow down and invest in others early on, we create memories today that will pay interest for years to come. Great leaders don't rush relationships. They invest in them.

> Great leaders don't rush relationships. They invest in them.

This is where the *Drip Effect* becomes more than a personal practice.

It becomes a cultural force.

When leaders *pause*, teams learn that reflection is valued.

When leaders *clarify*, teams learn to prioritize what matters.

When leaders *act* with purpose, teams move with confidence.

When leaders *refine*, teams learn that growth is expected—not avoided.

These aren't directives. They're signals. And people respond to what leaders signal, far more than what they say. Over time, those signals compound:

- A teacher begins to pause before reacting to a student.
- A team leader begins to ask better questions before making a decision.
- A staff member begins to take initiative instead of waiting for direction.

Not because they were told to. But because they experienced it. This is how leadership multiplies.

What Becoming Looks Like Over Time

Leadership doesn't change when behavior changes. It changes when capacity changes. And capacity is built, or depleted, by how leaders manage their margin.

You can adopt new strategies.
You can restructure your time.
You can try to "get ahead."

But if your margin is gone, your leadership will always default back to urgency. Becoming a *Drip Effect* leader doesn't happen in a single decision. It happens in small moments. Repeated over time. At first, it feels unnatural. For most leaders, speed has been rewarded. And slowing down can feel like falling behind. Not only does it feel like falling behind, but when you look around at others in person or on social media, you start to see what they are doing and stop seeing the work of who you are becoming. But over time, something begins to shift.

You *pause*—and realize not every moment requires a reaction.
You *clarify*—and see that not everything deserves your attention.
You *act*—and notice progress without exhaustion.
You *refine*—and begin learning faster than you are reacting.

Weeks pass. Then months. And the change becomes visible. Not just to you, but to the people around you. Meetings feel calmer. Conversations feel more honest. Decisions feel more grounded. And the pressure you once carried alone begins to distribute across the system.

Eventually, what once felt intentional becomes instinctive. You don't have to remind yourself to pause. You don't have to force clarity. You don't have to control every outcome. Because the way you lead has changed. And that's when you realize: You're no longer trying to apply the *Drip Effect*. You're leading from it.

The Rhythm You Return To

The Drip Effect is not four more things to do. It is a rhythm you return to when leadership becomes reactive instead of intentional—when speed starts making decisions for you. These rhythms protect leaders from becoming the kind of leader they never intended to be - always busy, but rarely present. *The Drip Effect* is how you return. Drop by drop. Most leaders start with movement. It's likely what got you to where you are today: the drive to fix, to serve, to make things better. And we commend you for that.

But lasting leadership doesn't come from *doing more*; it comes from *doing it with meaning* and *doing it well*. And if we are being open and honest, we want to do it well for you, and we hope *The Drip Effect* gives you a way to reclaim that meaning. It's not a program to complete or a checklist to master. It's a rhythm to live. A way of leading that quiets the noise, clarifies your purpose, and brings you back to who you are and want to be before you act and take on what's next.

When you are engaging in these rhythms you will regain moments of presence that were lost when you were in the hustle. Your focus will strengthen because of the depth of clarity you are finding. Trust amongst those you serve will deepen by your intentional actions. And by taking the time to earn the revisions you will develop a wisdom that you honestly didn't have time for before.

Over time, these drops accumulate and gain strength. They form patterns, systems, and relationships that don't rely on your constant push. They sustain themselves because they're built with meaningful intention. This is how you create calm in the midst of chaos. This is how you build teams that thrive, not just survive. This is how you stay grounded in who you are, even when everything around you demands speed. You don't have to change everything at once. You just have to begin, one pause, one choice, one drop at a time.

When you lead this way, your impact doesn't rush; it flows. And that's where you begin to experience real change.

A Final Invitation

Someday, you won't remember your to-do list. Your team and colleagues won't remember how quickly you responded to emails, how many initiatives you launched, or how many fires you put out on any given day. What they will remember are the moments that mattered:

- Did you notice them?
- Did you listen when it would have been easier to fix?

- Did you stay calm when everyone else panicked?
- Did you make people feel seen, heard, and valued?

That is the kind of leadership that lasts. It is not a final destination; it is a maintained skill. The type of skill you will need to help you see that there will always be fires to extinguish and initiatives to implement, but people evolve, and we must always keep them at the heart of our work. So here is our invitation as you close this book: Don't try to change everything tomorrow. Start with one drop:

- One *pause* before you respond.
- One *clarifying* question before you commit.
- One *act* of progress over perfection.
- One moment of *refinement* instead of self-criticism.

Who will you be long after the hustle fades? Let your leadership become meaningful, manageable, and sustainable, because leadership that isn't sustainable eventually becomes unsustainable for everyone. And when you inevitably fall back into sprinting (because we all do), don't spiral into guilt. Return to the rhythm:

Pause.
Clarify.
Act.
Refine.
Again. And again.

Until it's no longer something you practice— but who you are.

Who are you? Who do you want to be? What impact do you want to make?

That's the work. That's the win.

References

American Institute of Stress. (2025, January 3). *Redefining success in today's world of hustle culture.* https://www.stress.org/news/redefining-success-in-todays-world-of-hustle-culture/

Brooks, A. C. (2022). *From strength to strength: Finding success, happiness, and deep purpose in the second half of life.* Portfolio.

Cabeen, J. (2023). *Principal in Balance: Leading at Work and Living a Life.* Jossey-Bass.

Casas, J., & Birk, R. (2024). *Words on the wall: Culturizing your classroom for observable impact.* ConnectEDD.

Clear, J. (n.d.). *This coach improved every tiny thing by 1 percent.* https://jamesclear.com/marginal-gains

Fleming, C. M., Calvert, H. G., & Turner, L. (2024). Psychological safety among K-12 educators: Patterns over time, and associations with staff well-being and organizational context. *Psychology in the Schools, 61,* 2315–2337. https://doi.org/10.1002/pits.23165

Grant, A. (2021, April 19). There's a name for the blah you're feeling: It's called languishing. *The New York Times.* https://www.nytimes.com/2021/04/19/well/mind/covid-mental-health-languishing.html

Heath, D. (2020). *Upstream: The quest to solve problems before they happen.* Avid Reader Press.

Kahneman, D. (2011). *Thinking, Fast and Slow*. Farrar, Straus and Giroux.

Maslach, C., & Leiter, M. P. (2016). Understanding the burnout experience: Recent research and its implications for psychiatry. *World Psychiatry, 15*(2), 103–111. https://doi.org/10.1002/wps.20311

Mercurio, Z. (2023, October). *The cost of not mattering at work*. Zach Mercurio. https://www.zachmercurio.com/2023/10/the-cost-of-not-mattering-at-work

Motivational Stories (2017, March 15). The black dot. https://medium.com/motivationapp/the-black-dot-56fb02ee20cd

Parker, William D. (2020). PMP287: Chasing the Show with Pete Hall. *Principal Matters: The School Leader's Podcast*, 30. https://williamdparker.com/2022/pmp287-chasing-the-show-with-pete-hall/

Perkins, B. (2020). *Die with zero: Getting all you can from your money and your life*. Houghton Mifflin Harcourt.

Pura Vida [Film]. Martinez-Solares, 1956.

Polman, E., & Vohs, K. D. (2016). Decision fatigue, choosing for others, and self-construal. *Social Psychological and Personality Science, 7*(5), 471–478. https://doi.org/10.1177/1948550616639648

Sanfelippo, J. (2026). *Lead From Who You Are*. ConnectEDD Publishing.

Sutherland, R. (2020). *Alchemy: The surprising power of ideas that don't make sense*. WH Allen.

van der Steen, B., van Saane, J., & van Dijk, G. M. (2021). Leadership reflective practices: Adaptive challenges, slow questions and meaningful relations in fluid and accelerated times. *Journal of Studies in Social Sciences and Humanities, 7*(3), 233-241.

World Health Organization. (2021, May 17). *Long working hours increasing deaths from heart disease and stroke: WHO, ILO*. https://www.who.int/news/item/17-05-2021-long-working-hours-increasing-deaths-from-heart-disease-and-stroke-who-ilo

Acknowledgements

We are deeply grateful to our friends and colleagues who helped us turn our thoughts into words on a page, into the book you now hold in your hands. A sincere thank you to Brad Gustafson, Will Parker, Meg Simon, Joe Sanfelippo, Emily Graham, Taneka Tate, Courtney Dickey, and Jamie Downey, for your courage, vulnerability, wisdom, and thoughtful advice that not only challenged our thinking, but also strengthened this work along the way. Thank you to Jennifer Eakin Womble for her impactful opening foreword.

To each of our coaching clients—your commitment to be the best version of you, and your willingness to do the work continues to inspire us. You are the reason this message matters and we are truly honored to be a part of your life's work. We are forever grateful.

About the Authors

Jimmy Casas has been an educator for over 30 years, serving twenty-two years as a school leader. Under his leadership, his school was named one of the Best High Schools in the country three times by Newsweek and US News & World Report.

Jimmy was named the 2012 Iowa Secondary Principal of the Year and was selected as runner-up NASSP 2013 National Secondary Principal of the Year. In 2014, Jimmy was invited to the White House to speak on the Future Ready Schools pledge. Jimmy is also the author of ten books, including the Washington Post's best-selling book *CULTURIZE: Every Student. Every Day. Whatever It Takes*, which has sold over 350,000 copies to date.

Jimmy is the owner and CEO of J Casas & Associates, where he and his team serve as professional leadership coaches for school and district leaders across the country. In January 2020, Jimmy launched ConnectEDD, a publishing company aimed at giving back to the profession by supporting educators to become published authors. Connect with jimmy at jimmycasas.com

Dr. Jessica Cabeen is a principal, speaker, and leadership coach who challenges the pace of modern leadership with a simple concept: when you live well, you lead well.

She currently serves as Principal of Austin Online Academy and Austin Area Learning Center in Austin Public Schools (Minnesota). Across her career, she has led at every level of the system—as a middle school and kindergarten principal, special education assistant director, and special education teacher—bringing a grounded, practitioner's lens to her work with leaders.

Jessica is a Minnesota National Distinguished Principal and Principal of the Year by *Educational Dive*. She is the author of multiple books, including *Principal in Balance* and *Unconventional Leadership*, and co-author of *Balance Like a Pirate*. She is also a regular contributor to Edutopia and writes the "Slow Leadership" column on her blog.

When she's not greeting students at the door or holding office hours in the hallway, you'll find her with her husband, Rob, their sons Kenny and Isaiah, and their dogs, Herman and Harvey—living the same balance she challenges others to pursue. Connect with Jessica on her website at www.jessicacabeen.com.

More from
ConnectEDD Publishing

Since 2015, ConnectEDD has worked to transform education by empowering educators to become better-equipped to teach, learn, and lead. What started as a small company designed to provide professional learning events for educators has grown to include a variety of services to help educators and administrators address essential challenges. ConnectEDD offers instructional and leadership coaching, professional development workshops focusing on a variety of educational topics, a roster of nationally recognized educator associates who possess hands-on knowledge and experience, educational conferences custom-designed to meet the specific needs of schools, districts, and state/national organizations, and ongoing, personalized support, both virtually and onsite. In 2020, ConnectEDD expanded to include publishing services designed to provide busy educators with books and resources consisting of practical information on a wide variety of teaching, learning, and leadership topics. Please visit us online at connecteddpublishing.com or contact us at: info@ connecteddpublishing.com

Recent Publications:

Live Your Excellence: Action Guide by Jimmy Casas

Culturize: Action Guide by Jimmy Casas

Daily Inspiration for Educators: Positive Thoughts for Every Day of the Year by Jimmy Casas

Eyes on Culture: Multiply Excellence in Your School by Emily Paschall

Pause. Breathe. Flourish. Living Your Best Life as an Educator by William D. Parker

L.E.A.R.N.E.R. Finding the True, Good, and Beautiful in Education by Marita Diffenbaugh

Educator Reflection Tips Volume II: Refining Our Practice by Jami Fowler-White

Handle With Care: Managing Difficult Situations in Schools with Dignity and Respect by Jimmy Casas and Joy Kelly

Disruptive Thinking: Preparing Learners for Their Future by Eric Sheninger

Permission to be Great: Increasing Engagement in Your School by Dan Butler

Daily Inspiration for Educators: Positive Thoughts for Every Day of the Year, Volume II by Jimmy Casas

The 6 Literacy Levers: Creating a Community of Readers by Brad Gustafson

The Educator's ATLAS: Your Roadmap to Engagement by Weston Kieschnick

In This Season: Words for the Heart by Todd Nesloney, LaNesha Tabb, Tanner Olson, and Alice Lee

Leading with a Humble Heart: A 40-Day Devotional for Leaders by Zac Bauermaster

Recalibrate the Culture: Our Why…Our Work…Our Values by Jimmy Casas

Creating Curious Classrooms: The Beauty of Questions by Emma Chiappetta

Crafting the Culture: 45 Reflections on What Matters Most by Joe Sanfelippo and Jeffrey Zoul

Improving School Mental Health: The Thriving School Community Solution by Charle Peck and Dr. Cameron Caswell

Building Authenticity: A Blueprint for the Leader Inside You by Todd Nesloney and Tyler Cook

Connecting Through Conversation: A Playbook for Talking with Students by Erika Bare and Tiffany Burns

The Dream Factory: Designing a Purposeful Life by Mark Trumbo

Stories Behind Stances: Creating Empathy Through Hearing "The Other Side" by Chris Singleton

Happy Eyes: Becoming All Things to All People by Ryan Tillman

The Generative Age: Artificial Intelligence and the Future of Education by Alana Winnick

Recalibrate the Culture: Action Guide by Jimmy Casas

Leading with PEOPLE: A Six Pillar Framework for Fruitful Leadership by Zac Bauermaster

A School Leader's Guide to Reclaiming Purpose by Frederick C. Buskey

Foundations of an Elite Culture: Building Success with High Standards and a Positive Environment by David Arencibia

Personalize: Meeting the Needs of All Learners by Eric Sheninger and Nicki Slaugh

The Five Principles of Educator Professionalism: Rebuilding Trust in Schools by Nason Lollar

Words on the Wall: Culturizing Your Classroom For Observable Impact by Jimmy Casas and Cale Birk

School of Engagement: 45 Activities to Ignite Student Learning by Jonathan Alsheimer

Intentional Instructional Moves: Strategic Steps to Accelerate Student Learning by Sherry St. Clair

Overcoming Education: Complex Challenges, Difficult People, and the Art of Making a Difference by Brad R. Gustafson

The Language of Behavior: A Framework to Elevate Student Success by Charle Peck and Joshua Stamper

Whose Permission Are You Waiting For? An Educator's Guide to Doing What You Love by William D. Parker

The Leader You're Not…And Why It's Just As Important As the Leader You Are by Scott Borba

The Growth-Minded Leader by Tyler Cook

Day by Day: 180 Days of Hope and Encouragement by Zac Bauermaster

Make Your Move: For Ambitious People Ready to Live Their Aspirations by Marlon Styles, Jr.

The Hidden Work: What Separates Top Performers From Underachievers by Weston Kieschnick

Lifted to Lead: How a Paraplegic Orphan Rose from the Streets of Saigon to Become an American Leader by Stefan Bean and Kathy Nash

Lead From Who You Are: The Personal, People, and Process Rhythms of Meaningful Leadership by Joe Sanfelippo

Ready to Lead with AI: A Practical Guide for School Leaders by Kip Glazer

When All Means All: The Constellation of Learning Approach to Student-Centered Schools by Adam D. Drummond-Konopasek and Danny Drummond-Konopasek

A School Leader's Playbook for Tough Conversations by Erika Bare and Tiffany Burns

Expect! Engage! Empower! Three Pathways to Powerful Learning by Laurie Barron and Patti Kinney

www.ingramcontent.com/pod-product-compliance
Lightning Source LLC
Chambersburg PA
CBHW071434130726
47997CB00006B/2087